Humble Leadership

Humble Leadership

BEING RADICALLY OPEN TO GOD'S GUIDANCE AND GRACE

N. Graham Standish

THE
ALBAN
INSTITUTE

Herndon, Virginia
www.alban.org

The Alban Institute
2121 Cooperative Way, Suite 100
Herndon, VA 20171-5370

Unless otherwise noted, all Scripture quotations are from the New Revised Standard Version of the Bible, copyright © 1989, Division of Christian Education of the National Council of the Churches of Christ in the United States of America, and are used by permission.

Cover design by Concept Foundry.

Library of Congress Cataloging-in-Publication Data

Standish, N. Graham, 1959-
 Humble leadership : being radically open to God's guidance and grace / N. Graham Standish.
     p. cm.
 Includes bibliographical references.
 ISBN 978-1-56699-336-4
 1. Christian leadership. 2. Humility--Religious aspects--Christianity. I. Title.

 BV652.1.S68 2007
 253--dc22
                              2006103111

13   12   11   10   09   08   07   VG   1   2   3   4   5   6   7

Contents

Foreword

ONLY RARELY DOES A BOOK MAKE ME STOP, PUT IT DOWN, AND PRAY. From its opening pages to the very end, *Humble Leadership* made me do just that. Acting as a spiritual director, friend, and coach, Graham Standish draws readers into a deeper place to reflect upon their attitudes, motives, and practices of religious leadership.

Leadership is a popular topic with clergy and religious leaders—perhaps because so many ministers and church leaders feel challenged or inadequate when it comes to the task of leading their congregations and institutions. Especially in a time of cultural anxiety and change, when many churches are struggling for members, resources, and a renewed sense of mission, everyone recognizes that excellent leaders are needed. What kind of leaders can make a church successful? What practices make for good leaders? Does a particular leadership approach work better than others? Although many religious communities cry out for good leadership, there exists little agreement on what qualities make such leaders, resulting in conflicting expectations and agendas regarding leadership. Few topics cause more anxiety at clergy meetings or congregational gatherings, and more than a few ministers are tempted to give up on thinking about leadership. Yet, pastors' studies are often teeming with leadership books, mostly written for business leaders, and lay leaders often exercise church leadership in the exact same way they exercise leadership in their secular vocations. Leadership happens in church—and it usually happens in ad hoc, businesslike, and politicized ways.

Standish cuts through the fog of conflict, trendy approaches, and success-driven styles of leadership and poses a different set of questions. What makes for a *spiritual* leader? How can a leader draw others to God? What does leadership that is faithful and effective look like? He eschews leadership based on "business-like functionalism," a kind of leadership driven by quantifiable results. Instead, he delves into the tradition of Christian mysticism and draws out a historical narrative of *humble leadership*, a disposition of the soul that is "radically open to God's guidance and grace." This disposition creates an ability to move away from self-centered desires of power and control toward a genuine spiritual maturity that enables leaders to be appropriately self-aware, committed to others, and God-focused.

"Humble" and "leadership" may seem oxymoronic, but Standish argues that the Christian tradition has twinned the two—that from the desert fathers and mothers through medieval mystics to the Reformers and modern thinkers like Thomas Kelly, some of history's most passionate and effective spiritual leaders understood and demonstrated the power of humility in relation to their vocations to lead. Standish rightly points out that many transformative leaders held humility as a primary Christian virtue, the core virtue from which justice, compassion, and holiness spring. However, he also points out that most Christians, clergy included, rarely examine the nature, practice, and centrality of humility in their lives, much less in relation to leadership. Humility remains the most misunderstood of all the virtues, and in many ways it is the lost virtue. And that, Standish implies, may well be the problem with religious leadership.

But this book is not a critique of contemporary church leadership. Rather, it asks us to pray, reflect, and consider what the Christian virtue of humility means to our callings as leaders. Humble leadership invites us, as Standish writes, "to be strong in a wholly different and holy way." That way leads to a kind of "mystical intelligence," a new way of seeing, thinking, and understanding the practice of religious leadership and of participating in God's work in the world. Although this might sound like navel-gazing spirituality, something beyond the reach of busy pastors and regular church leaders, it is not. *Humble Leadership* is a practical book, full of relevant stories about both saints and normal church folk. Throughout, Standish unfolds helpful suggestions about spiritual direction, prayer, self-understanding, cultivating humor, discernment, and developing a rule of life. In addition to such personal disciplines, the final chapter connects theory with practice and outlines five specific skills for leaders in congregations.

Finally, I confess: Graham Standish is a friend, a person whom I respect deeply. I have watched him in action at Calvin Presbyterian and interviewed a number of people from Calvin Church for a project on vital congregations. *Humble Leadership* is more than theory; it is a way of life in a vibrant Christian community, a really good church in small-town America. This book comes from who Graham is—it combines his passions as a pastor, a student of Christian spirituality, a therapist, a storyteller, and a person of prayer. Although he is too humble to admit it, he practices what he preaches. It is easy to be skeptical about leadership, and even easier to be skeptical about someone writing about leadership, but I encourage you to practice what you read. Graham is an able guide and his book opens up a wise pathway into the territory of the soul. And do not be surprised if you have to put it down and pray.

Diana Butler Bass

Author, *The Practicing Congregation* and *Christianity for the Rest of Us*

Preface

CAN WE BE HUMBLE AND YET BE LEADERS? I HAVE BEEN CONSUMED by this question for a long time now. I've been curious about the connection between humility and leadership ever since I started reading the writings of mystics throughout Christian history. When I read their works, I was surprised at how often they talked about humility.

Of course, the emphasis on humility is as old as religion, and all religions emphasize it, but that doesn't mean that humility is practiced or stressed by religious folk in every age. Humility is an "essential" virtue that too many of the faithful forget is essential. In some ways, humility is the Sleeping Beauty of Christian virtues. It's often forgotten as it lies slumbering out of sight until certain courageous people decide to kiss it and in so doing awaken it and bring it back into the life of faith. Humility is among the hardest of all virtues because it requires that we willingly put aside ego and pride to embrace meekness. Who wants to do that? Putting aside ego and pride means letting our faith be created in God's image. It is much easier to mold faith to fit our image of what God wants. But humility won't let us do that.

I first became aware of how vital humility is to the Christian life in 1990 while studying the Christian mystics and spiritual masters as a doctoral student in spiritual formation. Reading their writings, I discovered that for the mystics, becoming humble was crucial. Why hadn't I ever heard that in my own religious upbringing? I had learned in church and seminary that virtues such as faith, hope, love, justice, peace, compassion, purity, and charity were what we were to strive for. I don't remember ever hearing a sermon or taking a class in which humility was stressed.

I was struck by how consistent these spiritual masters were in calling our attention to the importance of humility. For example, the Desert Fathers and Mothers of the fourth and fifth centuries, who imitated Christ's wilderness experience by living in the desert, believed that the desert taught them the essential lesson of humility. Living in the loneliness and desolation of the desert led them to struggle with their own demons. In the desert they discovered how powerless we humans really are, and this awareness helped them to let go of pride. In humility they learned to rely on God rather than on the mirage of their own power.

Another mystic, a sixth-century monk named Dorotheos of Gaza, taught that humility and self-accusation were central to the spiritual life. Francis of Assisi, in the 12th century, spoke often about the need to become humble before God. His life was a testimony to the power of humility. Catherine of Genoa, who cared for plague victims in the 15th century, said that God taught her that she could overcome her revulsion to the sores of plague victims by striving for humility. Thomas à Kempis, a priest who lived in the 14th and 15th centuries, wrote constantly about humility as more important than education and understanding. Luther and Calvin both saw the starting point of true faith as being a humble awareness of our own sin. The 20th-century mystics Evelyn Underhill, Thomas Kelly, Hannah Hurnard, Thomas Merton, and Henri Nouwen constantly emphasized a deepening humility as the pathway to spiritual growth.

I found similar instruction in Scripture. Blessed are the poor in spirit and the meek (Matt. 5:3, 5). The humble shall be exalted, and the exalted shall be humbled (Luke 18:14). To be great, we have to become humble like children (Matt. 18:3). In Philippians, Paul tells us to humbly think of others as better than ourselves (Phil. 2:3). In fact, the more aware I became of the need for humility, the more sensitive I became to how often humility is mentioned in Scripture.

As I learned more about humility, I kept wondering: why do modern Christians of all denominations and sects speak so little of humility? In fact, just the opposite seems to be true. It is not uncommon for Christians today to talk about wielding political and even military power on behalf of God. It is not unusual for contemporary Christians on the right and the left self-righteously to declare their position as "the correct" position and all opposing positions as wrongheaded or even heretical. Humility in leadership, to me at least, often seemed to be in short supply. Why had humility become the ugly duckling of all the Christian virtues?

As a pastor given the charge to lead a congregation, I wondered whether it was possible to be simultaneously humble and a leader. For a while, this question consumed me. In fact, one of the first pieces of writing I did for publication was an article titled "Can We Be Humble and Be Leaders?" It's a bit embarrassing to read the article today because my writing has improved, but rereading it, I see that I was on to something. I believed then and I believe now that we can reconcile the mystics' (who were leaders in their day) emphasis on humility with our modern understanding of leadership (which often ignores how powerful an ally humility can be for leaders). Prior to my reading of the mystics, I assumed what many in our culture assume: that cultivating a humble life gets in the way of leading a healthy and thriving organization. The mystics taught me that humility does not mean becoming feeble. Instead, it means bringing an attitude, a disposition of radical openness to God, into our leadership that allows us to become conduits of the Holy Spirit. The mystics demonstrated that to be humble actually means to be strong in a wholly different and holy way. It means to be strong in seeking God's way and then to have the courage to lead others in God's direction despite the resistance and outright opposition by those who want us to follow the ways of the culture and of convention. Humble leaders let Christ lead through them, guiding people to follow God's path.

Can we be humble and be leaders? That's the question I will explore in this book. From years of seeking an answer to this question and trying to lead from a humble foundation, I've discovered an answer. I do believe it is possible to be both humble and a leader. In fact, I believe that the best leaders always are humble; for it is out of their humility that they find a way to inspire, motivate, and unify those they lead.

My prayer for you is that in reading this book, you will discover a new and different way to lead: one based on first seeking God's way in everything and then on leading others toward God's goals.

1

Humble Leadership

—+— ≡◆≡ —+—

Therefore, to keep me from being too elated, a thorn was given me in the flesh, a messenger of Satan to torment me, to keep me from being too elated. Three times I appealed to the Lord about this, that it would leave me, but he said to me, "My grace is sufficient for you, for power is made perfect in weakness." So, I will boast all the more gladly of my weaknesses, so that the power of Christ may dwell in me. Therefore I am content with weaknesses, insults, hardships, persecutions, and calamities for the sake of Christ; for whenever I am weak, then I am strong.

2 Corinthians 12:7–10

IT WAS THE END OF MY FIRST YEAR OF SEMINARY. ALL OF MY FINAL PAPERS were written. All that remained was studying for my final exam in church history. As I sat down to review a semester's worth of material, something tugged at me. Let me rephrase that: something was calling me—a book sitting on my bed. I kept trying to study, but the book kept calling, saying, "Read me!" No, no, that's not right. The book wasn't calling me. God was calling me, telling me that reading the book would make more of an impact on my life and ministry than the church history exam. God wasn't saying that learning church history was unimportant. The message was deeper. It was as though God was saying that God would take care of the exam. I was to study something much more important for my own life and ministry.

What was the book on the bed? It was a biography of Mahatma Gandhi.[1] I had started the book a few days before as a diversion from my studies. From the first sentence, it affected me in a way that few other books have, before or since. It transformed

1

my life by changing my perspective on how we can serve God and lead others through prayer, humility, and faith. It's ironic that a biography of an Indian Hindu would have such an impact on an American Christian, but it shouldn't be surprising. Gandhi based much of his faith and life on Jesus, especially the Sermon on the Mount. In fact, he even considered becoming a Christian for a while, until he actually visited a church in South Africa. Filled with excitement after reading the Gospel of Matthew, he visited an Anglican church hoping to experience everything he had read. Upon entering the sanctuary, the usher, a white man, told him that he could not worship there because brown-skins like him weren't welcome. There was a church for his kind of people several miles away. Gandhi walked away from the church and Christianity that day but not from Christ. He remained determined to ground his life in the Christ he had discovered in the Bible.

What truly struck me was the way Gandhi led others. He led through humility. Gandhi had all the hallmarks of a humble leader. He led people both by becoming radically open to what God was calling him to do and by inviting others to follow in that direction. Humble leaders motivate people to follow *God's* vision. In contrast, conventional leaders motivate people to follow the leaders' vision. Leaders such as Gandhi voluntarily give up pride, arrogance, ego, and selfishness to become open to God's guidance and direction. Gandhi had a strength of character, conviction, vision, and faith that was amazing, yet it never led him to become prideful, arrogant, manipulative, or dismissive of others, especially of those who disagreed with him. Gandhi remained humble throughout his life, steeping his leadership in humility.

For example, in strategy meetings with fellow independence leaders, those with revered names such as Mohammed Ali Jinnah, Jawaharwal Nehru, and others, Gandhi surprised them and the servants by taking the tea set and serving them. In North American society this gesture may not seem so surprising, but in a society structured for over two millennia by a rigid caste system in which the ruling class simply didn't serve, it was scandalous. Serving the tea was an act of Christ, an act of leading others by serving them, an act rooted in Jesus's admonition in John 13 that to be a follower of him means to be a servant.

In another display of humble leadership, Gandhi shocked British and Indians alike by eschewing western clothing and wearing simple sarongs of homespun cotton. This act of humble defiance was his response to a British stranglehold on the Indian economy, the demand that only British-made textiles be produced and sold.

What was most astonishing, though, was Gandhi's willingness to suffer on behalf of others. While the leaders of most movements try to insulate themselves from suffering, Gandhi embraced it. He was always willing to put himself on the front line to receive beatings from his enemies. In South Africa, as a leader in the struggle for suffrage for those of Indian descent, Gandhi was willing to take a terrible beating from the constables, beatings that left him severely injured. He did so to demonstrate to other Indian expatriates that while their bodies could be broken, their spirit could not be killed. Gandhi led his fellow Indians into a peaceful rebellion in order to secure voting rights for all Indian immigrants.

When he returned to India, he led by setting a peaceful, God-focused example. He invited others to protest the British through nonviolent confrontation. He believed that nonviolence was a powerful weapon. And when the Indian people became violent in their protests, Gandhi embarked upon a personal hunger strike by fasting for weeks. His intent was to strike not against the British but against the Indian people. He deeply believed that the use of violence by the Indian people gave legitimacy to the British by giving them just cause to crush revolts violently. When they remained nonviolent, provoking British violence, they gave legitimacy to the Indian people by demonstrating that the British were unjust. So Gandhi fasted until the Indian people halted all violence. He promised them that he would fast and pray unto death unless all violence against the British ended. As a leader, Gandhi led the Indian people to adhere to Jesus's teaching: "Love your enemies, do good to those who hate you, bless those who curse you, pray for those who mistreat you. If someone strikes you on one cheek, turn to him the other also" (Luke 6:27–29). As a Hindu, Gandhi may not have been a practicing Christian, but his principles as a leader were thoroughly Christian.

Gandhi led from a strength rooted in humility, and I learned from him that there is a power in humility. I learned from Gandhi that leading from humility makes allies even of enemies. It is said that upon receiving a present of a simple, homespun cotton sarong Gandhi himself had made, the Earl of Mountbatten told the king of England that this cloth should be locked in the tower of London with the British crown jewels. This was the respect that Gandhi garnered even from an enemy, an enemy who had a profound respect and love for Gandhi.

I learned a lot from Gandhi. I learned that humble leadership exposes self-interest and selfishness in both enemies and friends alike, as it simultaneously purifies motives. When we lead from a sense of humility, willingly putting aside our own motivations and desires in favor of God's call, we create the context in which people are more willing to put aside their own will to seek God's will.

I also learned that whatever we are doing, humble leadership allows us to find the path to greater creativity and possibility in whatever we are doing. Gandhi demonstrated, time and time again, how humility enables us to discern creative solutions. His solutions to apparent problems and obstacles were ingeniously creative—and creativity made his nonviolent path toward Indian independence a powerful force. The British could never anticipate what he was going to do. Still, Gandhi never led capriciously. He steeped his plans in prayer. For instance, at one point the Indian independence movement was stalling. There was tremendous pressure for Gandhi to do something, *anything*, to get the movement back on track. Gandhi did something, but it was not what his followers expected. They wanted quick, decisive action. Gandhi gave them prayer.

Gandhi spent eight months at his ashram, a commune-like religious community, praying and seeking God's will despite pleas from millions that he do something. Suddenly one day as he sat by a pond, he received God's answer. He told his followers to pack their things, to join him in prayer, and to prepare to act. After dinner and worship, Gandhi and his supporters began to walk. Day after day he walked through towns and villages, and many of the villagers joined the procession. Gandhi kept silent about their destination and objective until he stopped at the sea. With thousands of followers now behind him and many British soldiers surrounding him, he walked calmly to the edge of the water where a large chunk of salt had been formed by the evaporation of water in the hot Indian sun. He picked up the salt, walked over to a British soldier, and said, "I have manufactured salt. You must arrest me!"

So what? Why was this so important? It was important because in this small chunk of salt Gandhi had found a symbol of Indian freedom. A few years earlier, in another attempt to maintain power over the Indian economy, the British had made it illegal for Indians to manufacture this essential element. Only the British could manufacture salt. In a simple gesture, Gandhi had shown the absurdity of British law in India by presenting the British with a dilemma. If they arrested Gandhi, they would reveal the oppressiveness of their laws to the Indian people, the British population, and the world. If they didn't arrest him, they would give implicit permission to the whole Indian population to defy the British in this and every other economic concern. They arrested Gandhi, but his imprisonment ended up giving freedom to the Indians as millions made their own salt by pouring seawater into pans and letting it evaporate on their rooftops.

Gandhi demonstrated to Christians the power of the gospel; he showed how leaders grounded in Christ can transform hearts, minds, souls, and nations when they are willing to become humble leaders. Gandhi also revealed how dangerous humble leadership can be. It can expose the falseness and hypocrisy of the world's ways. Humble leaders can show people how to experience and follow God in ways they never expected, a pilgrimage that transforms them in ways that they may not anticipate or always welcome. At the same time, humble leadership can be personally dangerous to those of us who seek this humble way. It exposes us to our own weakness, powerlessness, fear, and anxiety. It is impossible to be a humble leader and not grapple constantly with these forces. The way of humility invites us to follow God's path, a path that potentially leads to failure—the failure to achieve our ambitions through strength in a world that worships power. When we lead through humility, we are choosing a path that emphasizes meekness and weakness, leaving us open to the manipulations of those devoted to wielding power. If we are to become humble leaders, we have to develop a different kind of strength. This strength is a strength of character that few are willing to form, a strength of the Spirit that has its roots in Christ's way rather than the world's way. I can think of nothing more humbling than to discover the power of humble leadership from a man like Mahatma Gandhi, who had been rejected by Christians yet lived the gospel more profoundly than most Christians ever will.

I learned a lot about humble leadership from Gandhi. I also learned another important lesson by reading his biography rather than spending hours studying church history. I learned that if we trust and follow God's call, the Spirit takes care of us. I went into the exam feeling ill prepared. I also went in knowing that I had been called to study Gandhi rather than the Reformation. When the exams were passed out, I looked down at the multiple choice, true/false questions. I knew the answers to about 50 percent of them. I guessed on the rest. When I received my grade a week later I had been given an A. Chills went down my spine. I don't want to give the impression to any students that we should read biographies of Gandhi instead of studying for exams. This was a special experience, never repeated. I felt a call to study a life rather than a subject, and I discovered that when we humbly do what Christ calls us to do, God finds a way to make things work out in the end. This was the ultimate lesson I learned from my experience with Mahatma Gandhi. When we humble ourselves as we lead others, God works through us to do Christ's will. By aligning our will with God's, we invite the Spirit's power to flow through us and into whatever congregation or organization we are leading.

THE CONSPIRACY AGAINST HUMILITY

For a variety of reasons, a definite bias against humility resides in modern culture. Resistance to humility has always been part of the human fabric, but modern Western culture—like all cultures that become highly developed educationally, economically, and militarily—seems to be especially resistant to humility. As Americans, we live in a strong and powerful culture that associates humility with weakness, spinelessness, and even cowardice. Our cultural need for strength infects Christian leadership with a pride that causes Christian leaders to ignore biblical teachings about grounding our lives in humility. The irony is that as an emphasis on biblically grounded Christianity grows among evangelical Christians, an emphasis that influences the writings of many on Christian leadership, attention to humble leadership appears to be decreasing. I see this trend in the demeanor and statements of such prominent evangelicals as Jerry Falwell, Pat Robertson, and others like them who continually emphasize the need to wield power on God's behalf. Whether it is Jerry Falwell, preaching during the lead-up to the Iraq invasion that we should shoot a cruise missile with Saddam Hussein's name on it into Baghdad to kill him, or Pat Robertson's suggestion that we should assassinate the Venezuelan president, I see little humility in their leadership.

Looking at what the Bible says about the Christian life, we see that humility ranks among the most important virtues. For example, in Proverbs it is said, "Pride only brings quarrels, but wisdom is found in those who take advice" (13:10), and "Haughty eyes and a proud heart, the lamp of the wicked, are sin!" (21:4). Moses, one the greatest leaders of the Old Testament, led from humility. We often think of Moses as a powerful and charismatic leader, but that's an image created in movies, not in the Bible. When God first calls Moses to lead the Israelites out of Egypt, Moses responds by saying, "Who am I, that I should go to Pharaoh and bring the Israelites out of Egypt?" (Exod. 2:10). Moses constantly peppers God with questions about how to get others to follow. Moses often responds to God by asking, "What if they do not believe me or listen to me and say, 'The Lord did not appear to you'?" When he is told to share the message of God with the people of Israel, Moses says to God, "O Lord, I have never been eloquent, neither in the past nor since you have spoken to your servant. I am slow of speech and tongue." These are hardly the words of a confident, strong, and prideful leader. They are the words of a humble leader. In fact, although Moses may have been a proud man in his youth, by the time God calls him he is a broken, frightened shepherd in the desert. This is no king. Moses is a simple man who has learned to be humble in the harshness of the desert.

In biblical tradition, the desert is where most of God's leaders learn humility. Those wandering in the desert suffer thirst, hunger, loneliness, and confusion. They face themselves—including their weaknesses, delusions, and failures. They have no power in the desert as they grovel and struggle to remain alive. These experiences become the preconditions for finally humbling ourselves before God. We recognize that little hope lies in our own power. The shepherd Moses discovered this truth when he lived in the desert for 40 years. He had been powerful in Egypt, but in the desert he was powerless. And this weakness opened him to God.

Jesus also pointed out the importance of humility in his teachings. He didn't emphasize strength and the use of force to lead people but rather humility and meekness. What are we supposed to do to our enemies? Bless them, pray for them, and do good to them (Luke 6:27). Whom are we supposed to emulate? Certainly not the Pharisees, who take pride in their religious practice and righteousness. We are to emulate the sinful tax collector who will not even look up to heaven, but beats his breast, and says to God, "Lord, have mercy on me, a sinner" (Luke 18:9–14). According to Jesus, to be great we have to become like children (9:46–48); we have to be willing to bear our crosses (14:27); and we have to willingly become servants to all (John 13:1–17).

Looking at the epistles of Paul, we see the same message echoed. In a passage particularly mystifying for modern Christians who identify faith with strength, Paul tells us that he was afflicted with an infirmity that God would not remove. God's response to Paul's pleas is "My grace is sufficient for you, for my power is made perfect in weakness" (2 Cor. 12:9). Paul, the great leader of the early church, concludes, "Therefore I will boast all the more gladly about my weaknesses, so that Christ's power may rest on me. That is why, for Christ's sake, I delight in weaknesses, in insults, in hardships, in persecutions, in difficulties. For when I am weak, then I am strong" (2 Cor. 12:9–10). This passage is rarely cited by Christian leaders as a model for leadership. Why not?

The answer is that humans have a natural lust for power. Is it a remnant of our more primitive days when survival was all that mattered, when gaining and maintaining power meant living a longer life, obtaining more possessions, and building a greater sense of security? Actually, it's not only a remnant. Concern for survival and security lies at the heart of our lives even today and contributes to human sin. Much of human sin has to do with focusing on ourselves and our survival while we simultaneously ignore God and the welfare of others. We all want a better chance at survival and greater security, and these desires prompt some to be consumed with achieving their ambitions, gaining control, and wielding power in the drive to be successful, often to the point of sinfully caring only about themselves, not others, not God. The drive of ambition is a large part of modern-day ministry as evidenced by those whom we identify as successful pastors. In mainline and evangelical publications, seminars, and workshops, the pastors cited as successes and models are the ones who have taken new churches and led their growth to phenomenal sizes: 5,000, 10,000, 15,000, 20,000 members. How many pastors measure themselves according these standards, and how many wish they had that kind of success? Here we see evidence of our ambition. Ambition is often a stronger force than a desire to serve God.

We church leaders often feel torn. We don't always know what or whom we are serving: our own basic desires for power and success, or God. It is easy to confuse the two, especially when we seek to gain or wield power on behalf of God. If we seek to be successful in ministry, are we motivated by a desire to please God or to be identified as a success? It is hard to ascertain what motivates us. As a result, many serve themselves in their ministries rather than God. Of course, the reality of human sin is that our motives will never be completely pure, but the more we seek the humble way, the clearer we become that the desire to please God, not the desire to be a success, is our motivation.

A modern style of leadership has developed that leaves little room for humility. It is a functional style of leadership grounded in goal setting, quantifiable strategies for achieving goals, accountability, hierarchy, structure, and measurable results. All of these tactics are based on human analysis, logic, and planning, which can be used to lead people effectively in God's direction. The problem with the functional style of leadership arises when the use of these strategies causes leaders to ignore the primary element of Christian leadership: humbly seeking God's will. Functional leadership tactics, because they emanate from human-oriented strategies, can cause us to mistake our desires and goals for what God wants both for us and for our churches.

I saw this kind of functional leadership in a pastor I knew who confused his own ambitions with God's will. He was a skillful preacher, a man with vision and drive as well as a a genuine desire to lead people to serve Christ. Yet a primary problem hampered his leadership. He made the tragic assumption that he was the only one in the church who understood what God wanted, and he became increasingly bitter as the church resisted his vision, plans, and programs. He would complain that his congregation was constantly resisting him and undermining his authority. He would lament that the members of his congregation were defiant, continually trying to subvert him. Eventually he left the congregation and active ministry, probably only months before he would have been pushed out of the congregation anyway. His whole style of leadership was one that is typical of too many modern leaders. He made the prideful assumption that because he was seminary-trained, he was closer to God and therefore knew what the congregation should be doing. When the congregation didn't follow immediately, he assumed that they were resisting and subverting his plans. The church made him miserable, and he made the members miserable. Unfortunately, too many churches are plagued by this kind of leadership. Too many churches have pastoral and lay leaders who are somewhat arrogant, assuming they always know what is best and that the members are spiritual infants who are ignorant of God's desires.

The sixth-century monk and mystic Dorotheos of Gaza gives amazing guidance, not only about how to be a Christian, but also how to be a Christian leader. He eventually became a leader

in his brotherhood, an order of monks who lived harsh and as-
cetic lives in the deserts of Palestine. Dorotheos went through
some humbling times, enduring the slings and arrows of fellow
monks who were critical of him and who often did things to torment him, like shaking their mats in his hut (to attract stinging
insects). Dorotheos's response? He blamed himself, not them, for
their reaction to him. He taught that humility is grounded in ac-
cusing ourselves, rather than others, for failures. As he says:

> Don't you see that this is why we make no progress, why we
> find that we have not been helped towards it? We remain all the
> time against one another, grinding one another down. Because
> each considers himself right and excuses himself, as I was say-
> ing, all the while keeping none of the Commandments yet ex-
> pecting his neighbor to keep the lot! This is why we do not ac-
> quire the habits of virtue, because if we light on any little thing
> we tax our neighbor with it and blame him saying he ought not
> to do such a thing and why did he do it—whereas ought we
> not rather to examine ourselves about the Commandments and
> blame ourselves for not keeping them?[2]

What's the connection between this self-accusation and leadership? Too many leaders assert their own egos and blame others
for not following where they lead. Dorotheos offers an amazing
contrast by encouraging people to take responsibility for their
failures instead of blaming others. But if you are like most Americans, what Dorotheos says seems foreign and impractical. How
are we supposed to lead from a stance of self-accusation and humility? To gain an understanding, it might be helpful to stop and
consider what humility is, rather than what we think it is.

WHAT IS HUMILITY?

For many Christians, Darwin's theory of evolution is a problem,
but I believe social Darwinism, the theory that only the strong
deserve to rule, is a more serious threat. As a result of this mindset, many in our culture can't even conceive how there could be

anything positive about being humble, because humility seems to promote helplessness. We are a people who believe in survival of the fittest, at least on a social level, believing that any sign of vulnerability is an admission of failure. The whole idea of humility seems impractical.

This survival-of-the-fittest perspective is so pervasive that it has become inherent in the leadership in many of our churches. Too many pastors and lay leaders get caught up in unnecessary power struggles as they vie with each other for control. For example, many smaller churches—family- or pastoral-sized churches with an average attendance under 150—have trouble keeping pastors because of these power struggles. This is especially a problem in family-sized congregations (congregations with an average Sunday attendance of 49 or less) in which a lay member has amassed a tremendous amount of power and engages any new pastor in a struggle for control. Usually the power struggles cause the pastor (often a recent seminary graduate serving in his or her first call) to leave the congregation within three years. In some cases, this experience can devastate a pastor enough to cause her or him to leave ministry entirely. On the surface the issue may be the theology of the pastor, whether the pastor is visiting the members enough, or how the pastor dresses, but at deeper levels the issue is power—who should have it and who does have it. The lay member feels threatened by the pastor and finds some reason to get congregants to choose sides in the conflict, which they do, usually siding with the lay member.

At the same time the pastor may feel threatened by a lay leader's power. On the surface the issue may be the lay leader's lack of faith, resistance to the pastor's leadership, or subversive nature, but at deeper levels the issue is power. The pastor wants power that he feels the lay leader has.

Perhaps the problem we have today isn't with humility, but with our understanding of humility. We don't understand what humility is. The concept of humility is grounded in the story of Genesis and is a thread woven throughout the fabric of the Bible. Humility is grounded in our creation. According to Genesis, the first human, Adam, is created out of *adamah*, or dirt. The word "human" comes from the Latin for dirt, *humus*. To become humble means, first, to recognize our earthiness, our dirt-ness, our creation from dust. Humility is a recognition that we are made of the same stuff as the rest of the universe. We are nothing but carbon molecules strung together in a human matrix.

We are distinct and special not because of any qualities or abilities we ourselves possess. Our unique qualities are gifts from God that come from God's Spirit breathed into us. This is the second part of understanding humility—that what makes us unique is nothing we do by our own power, but only what God has given us through the gift of the Holy Spirit. According to Genesis, God formed the first human "from the dust of the ground, and breathed into his nostrils the breath of life; and the man became a living being" (Gen. 2:7). The Hebrew word for "breath of life" is *ruach*, which also means God's Spirit. In essence, the breath of life is God's Spirit, which God has breathed into us. In the Genesis story, humans are the only creatures that have had the Spirit breathed into them. All other creatures are given life but not Spirit. Humans are endowed with a spirit that allows them to transcend their created nature. Transcendence is a gift from God, and it alone sets us apart from the rest of creation.

This gift of God's Spirit, God's breath, allows us to transcend our animal nature and become self-aware and self-reflective, abilities that other animals don't have. This gift of Spirit allows us to make free choices about how we will live our lives, when all other animals are ruled by instinct and drive. This gift of Spirit allows us to challenge ourselves and strive to exceed our limitations while other animals are simply stuck following their genetic packaging and social conditioning. Finally, this gift allows us to be aware of and to experience God, which no other animals can do. From this perspective we also begin to see the connection between pride and sin. Sin emerges as we cultivate the belief that our uniqueness is due to our own efforts independent of God. We fail to recognize God's Spirit in us, God's gift of life and awareness. Humility begins the process of restoring us to an appreciation of God's gift of Spirit and life, whose effect is to enable us to grow in Spirit.

From the perspective of Genesis, humility isn't weakness. It is awareness and appreciation of the fact that we are made of earth and Spirit, and that it is the *Spirit* part of us that gives us our creativity, our abilities, our insights, and our skills. Without Spirit we are nothing but dead matter. The humble person sees her abilities as a gift from God, not as evidence of personal greatness.

So what is humility? From a Genesis perspective it is an awareness and appreciation that we are a combination of dust and spirit, with the Spirit both giving us life and connecting us with God and God's will.

Humility is grounded also in the teachings of Jesus. At a basic level, all of Jesus's teachings show us how to choose the humble way rather than the way of pride, the tendency to place ourselves at the center of universe. When we are prideful, we become selfish and self-focused, rather than loving and God-focused, and we believe we are special because of our own talents, abilities, looks, or insights. Looking at the teachings of the Sermon on the Mount (Matt. 5:1–12) we can see the difference between the prideful and humble ways of living. The blessed are those who mourn; those who are poor in spirit, meek, cursed, persecuted, and pure in heart; those who are peacemakers. These are the humble. The cursed are the rich, the full, the laughing, and the honored (Luke 6:24–26). Jesus identifies these people because they are living lives that can easily lead them to fall into the trap of pride.

Throughout the Gospels, Jesus teaches people how to live in humility by loving others, especially enemies, giving generously, praying regularly, refusing to let anxiety rule their lives, respecting others rather than judging them, relying on God's grace, seeking the narrow way of surrender to Christ, and much more (Matt. 6–7). For Jesus, the great are those who are humble like children (18:1–4). As I mentioned earlier, Jesus's example of the righteous person is not the proud Pharisee who follows the law perfectly, but the humble and sinful tax collector who will not look to heaven but, groveling on the ground, says to God, "Have mercy on me, a sinner" (Luke 18:9–14). Of this man, Jesus says, "I tell you that this man, rather than the other, went home justified before God." Jesus's teachings demonstrate that humility opens us to grace and blessings. Interestingly, the story of the Pharisee and the tax collector adds a new perspective on justification. We have been taught that we are justified by grace through faith, but this parable suggests that we are justified by grace *through humility;* for as Jesus says about the humble tax collector, "I tell you, this man went down to his home justified rather than the other" (Luke 18:14).

Looking at how central the concept of humility seems to be in Jesus's teaching, we can add to our definition that humility is the awareness and appreciation of our earthiness and Spirit-ness. Humility is also our willingness to act in ways that are other- and God-focused rather than self-focused.

Jesus is also the model of humility. Before embarking on his ministry, he does something completely surprising. Having just been baptized and filled with the Holy Spirit, he goes out into the desert for 40 days and nights to fast, suffer, and be tempted. Who among us would have the humility to do that? Most of us, emboldened and empowered by the Holy Spirit, would rush ahead ready to change the world. In contrast, Jesus humbly goes into the desert. In going into the desert, Jesus was doing more than being obedient. Obedience to God arises out of law, as we seek to fulfill God's commands. Humility leads us beyond obedience. We become Spirit-guided as we begin to do what God wills through us. Humility leads to a radical openness to God whereby we allow God's Spirit both to guide us and work through us.

Jesus's humility was evidenced in his willingness to follow the leading of the Spirit, rather than his own insights and desires. Instead of trying to change the world all at once, he journeyed into the desert to become united with the Father and Holy Spirit. The desert, throughout the Bible, is the place where people of faith and power learn the way of humble service to God. Adam, Abraham, Moses, Elijah, David, the Israelites, Paul, and many others learned humility in the desert—a place with little more than dirt that reconnected them with their "earthiness." Jesus humbly followed the Spirit into the desert, and his humble following of the Spirit became a grounding for his leadership. He led by following the Spirit to lead others to follow the Spirit.

So we now add a third dimension to our definition of humility. To be a humble leader means to follow willingly wherever the Spirit leads, and to make following the Spirit, even into times of struggle and dryness, the ground from which we lead others to follow the Spirit.

Jesus teaches us that to be a humble leader means to be a servant leader. A humble leader is one who is literally and figuratively ready to wash the feet of those who are considered to be less than us: "Now that I, your Lord and Teacher, have washed your feet, you also should wash one another's feet. I have set you an example that you should do as I have done for you. I tell you the truth, no servant is greater than his master, nor is a messenger greater than the one who sent him. Now that you know these things, you will be blessed if you do them" (John 13:14–17). To be humble, then, also means being a servant.

So what is humility? Considering all that we have said, humility begins with an awareness of what we are without God, and that all that is unique about us comes as a gift from God. Humility is also the willingness to become God- and other-focused rather than being narcissistically self-focused. It means willingly following the guidance of the Spirit wherever it leads. Finally, it means becoming a servant of God and others. All of these aspects of humility are reflected in the writings of the Quaker mystic and writer Thomas Kelly, who says:

> But humility rests upon a holy blindedness, like the blindedness of him who looks steadily into the sun. For wherever he turns his eyes on earth, there he sees only the sun. The God-blinded soul sees naught of self, naught of personal degradation or personal eminence, but only the Holy Will working impersonally through him, through others, as one objective Life and Power.... But the humility of the God-blinded soul endures only so long as we look steadily at the Sun. Growth in humility is a measure of our growth in the habit of the Godward-directed mind. And he only is near to God who is exceedingly humble.[3]

Humility, in the end, is a state of being in which we willingly try to seek and serve God's will in everything. We do our best to discern God's will and follow it, and in the process, we willingly set aside, to the extent possible, everything that gets in the way. The irony is that sometimes even religion, and especially theological education, can be one of those obstacles to humility. As the great 15th-century mystic Thomas à Kempis wrote:

What good does it do, then, to debate about the Trinity, if by a lack of humility you are displeasing to the Trinity? In truth, lofty words do not make a person holy and just, but a virtuous life makes one dear to God.... Everyone naturally wishes to have knowledge, but what good is great learning unless it is accompanied by a feeling of deep awe and profound reverence toward God? Indeed, a humble farmer who serves God is better than a proud philosopher, who, neglecting himself, contemplates the course of the heavens.[4]

HUMBLE LEADERSHIP AS OPENNESS TO GOD

Traditionally, humility is understood as a virtue. And humility is a Christian virtue because, like all other virtues, the practice of humility opens us to Christ's presence; or more specifically, it enables us to pay attention to Christ's presence and guidance. Humility orients us more toward the spiritual so that we can live a life of Spirit. Another way to understand humility is to view it as a state of being in which we become radically open to God throughout our lives. Humility is a way of life in which we become consumed with seeking God's direction rather than living purely according to our instincts, conditioning, and insights. For the Christian, humility integrates our spiritual and human natures in a way that allows us to become united with Christ.

If humility enables us to develop a radical openness to God throughout our lives, humble leadership means leading others with that openness. As humble leaders we work to develop an ever-deepening awareness of where God is leading us and then lead others in that direction. We lead from openness so that we can lead others toward that openness. In some ways this process is similar to playing jazz, a form of music that demands openness by both players and audience.

I discovered the connection between jazz and humble openness from a musician friend. He said that you cannot be arrogant when you play jazz. Even if the musician is the leader of the band, he cannot be egotistical, because ego kills the spirit of the music. Jazz is about being open to the power of the music. The jazz musician follows a basic musical rhythm and theme. Then, when it is time for his solo, he does his best to become open to the spirit of the song. When another musician solos, he then lays back and supports that solo as faithfully as he performed his own.

I asked him whether he practiced ahead of time what he was going to play. He had a simple answer: "Oh no! To practice my solo ahead of time means to be arrogant. It assumes that I can figure out ahead of time what God wants me to play. I consider jazz music to be like a prayer, and when it comes time for me to play my prayer, I need to be completely open to see where I'm being led. It's a real spiritual thing." This last sentence sums up humble leadership. Humble leadership is a radical, prayerful openness to God, as God guides us to lead people to experience what God is already preparing.

When we are humble leaders, we grow increasingly comfortable with the uncertainty that comes with trying our best to be available to God and God's guidance. Ultimately, humility and humble leadership are about choosing whether we will be open or closed to God. The choice is reflected in the figure on the next page.

We are taught as Christians that we have freedom of choice in our lives, but do we really? What kinds of choices do we really have? Can I choose to be Chinese? Can I choose to be in two places at once? Or three, or four, or a hundred? Can I really choose my destiny? We really don't have much choice about many of the most important things in life, and most of us know it. We are confined by national, ethnic, familial, cultural, societal, psychological, social, economic, and educational constraints. How much can we really choose in life?

The basic problem that we humans have is that while we are spiritual beings with a spiritual nature—a nature that, according to Christian doctrine, leads us to freedom of choice—we are also animals with an animal nature. The animal nature urges us to live captive to instinct, urges, drives, and desires. As humans we have been given the gift of choice from God to determine which nature will be the strongest influence in our lives: the animal or the spiritual. Each of us is given the freedom to choose the extent to which we will be open or closed to God in each moment of life. We can choose whether to be constrained by our animal nature

HUMBLE LEADERSHIP

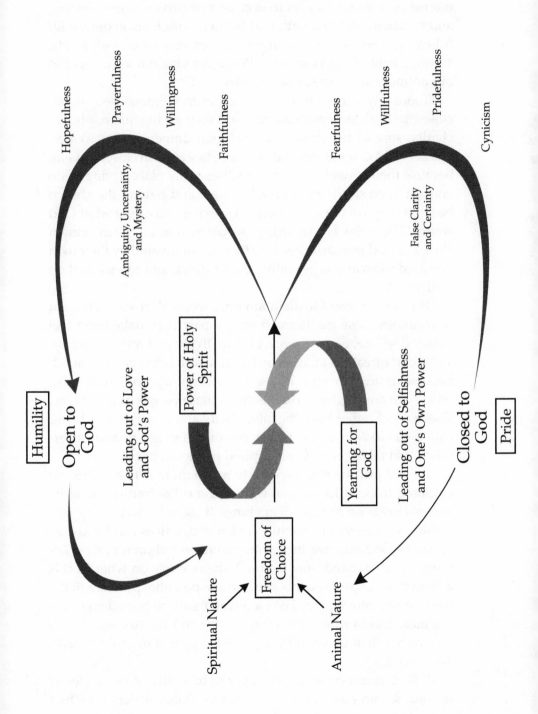

or freed by our spiritual nature. Abandoning ourselves to our animal nature confines us to serving our drives, urges, desires, and instincts, and to a path that is filled with fear, anxiety, willfulness (a need to be in charge), and an obsession with safety, security, control, and certainty. When we give ourselves over to our animal nature, we close ourselves to God.

Too many people in our culture, even religious people, are closed to God. It doesn't matter that they go to church, give to charity, sing in the choir, attend church dinners and activities, and serve on committees and boards. They are still closed to God, because their focus is more on creating a safe place, trying to do enough good deeds to get into heaven, and having the church be what they want it to be, than on seeking and doing what God wants. The point is that many people within a church remain closed to God primarily because they are motivated by their own deeper desires and urges rather than by an intent to seek and do God's will.

People who want to maintain tradition at all costs often want to maintain those traditions from the past that make them feel safe and secure, and they react instinctively and angrily to anything that threatens their security. They resist change in a church because change means living in uncertainty and ambiguity, which are among the worst feelings these people can imagine. They would rather have the false clarity and certainty that being closed to God provides, rather than the ambiguity and uncertainty that taking new, God-inspired paths can bring.

It's not just members trying to maintain traditions who can be closed to God. Those who want to get rid of traditions can be just as closed off to God. Sometimes those who want only *new* music, *new* orders of worship, and *new* practices can be just as closed to God because they want to create a church that serves them and their needs, not a church that focuses on what God is calling them to do. I see this attitude as a potential problem in the megachurch movement. The focus can easily be placed on creating monuments to the founding pastor and his (usually "his") ego, rather than on creating a place for people to grow in faith and Christ.

Just as members of the church can be guilty of being closed to God, so can pastoral and lay leaders These leaders may fear the confusion and possible conflict that openness to God might bring. Why bother introducing new music, programs, ways of "being church" if it is going to tick people off? Better to keep doing what we've always done to remain secure, even if remaining stable and secure will eventually lead to the church's demise. Of course, they don't say it this way. In their minds they see themselves as defenders of tradition and guardians of theological truth and purity. Many of these leaders close themselves off so that they can seek their own desires and goals. They lead from selfishness and a desire to wield power. This is a common problem, especially as more and more church leaders come under the sway of church gurus who make adding members and growing in numbers the main goal of the church. The critical question is "What is God's will?" not "What do our ambitions, fears, and drives lead us to do?" It is possible to do the things that promote church growth with little consideration for what God wants. All it takes is the right marketing strategy, an engaging and entertaining worship service, and educational and training programs that attract folk who are spiritual hungry and don't care what kind of spiritual food they get—as long as it tastes good.

The mainline church today suffers a crisis of creativity because we have too many leaders who are closed to God. They hide their spiritual congestion behind theological justifications and tradition, offering compelling arguments for never changing worship, keeping church practices sacrosanct, and complaining that the general population is so shallow that it fails to appreciate the power of traditional liturgy. There may be kernels of truth in what they say, but it all conceals the fact that they have no interest in seeking God's will. What if God wants us to change our worship? What if God is calling us to update our practices? What if God is calling us to try new things? What if God is calling us to do what we've always done, but in nuanced ways that attract new members? It's always easier to close ourselves off to God's will. That way we also avoid confusion, uncertainty, and potential conflict with members who have a vested interest in keeping things the same.

A similar set of questions may also be appropriate for devotees of the new worship tradition—contemporary worship. Contemporary worship has been around long enough that it has

become a sacred cow in some circles. Proponents of contemporary worship often regard the emergent church movement—a
movement emphasizing the recapturing of ancient traditions and
practices and integrating them with contemporary worship—as
being almost sacrilegious. What if God is calling them to change
their worship? What if God is calling them to nuance what they
are doing and to try new things, which might mean a return to
the traditional and the ancient?

So what is the nature of humble leadership? It is leadership
that is radically open to God—in which we lead from faith rather
than fear, from a willingness to let God's will flow through us
rather than willfully insisting that our own will be done, from
hope rather than cynicism, from love rather than selfishness, and
from God's power rather than our own power. When we lead
with an openness to God, we allow God's power and grace to
flow through us. We make prayer and discernment a foundation
of our leadership, always seeking first what God wants and then
leading others in that direction by inviting them to the same kind
of humble prayer and discernment.

This is not an easy path, because it feels ambiguous and uncertain. There are no guarantees when we choose to lead with
openness. Why? Because it's leadership that arises from discerning God's path, and discernment is never easy. When we are open
to God, we run the risk of traveling through deserts and valleys
of shadows. The vision may not be clear, and not everyone will
follow us. When we close ourselves off to God and follow tried-
and-true paths, vision and programs seem much clearer and easier because we follow where others have already trod. Becoming
open to God and leading with openness can be troubling. What
if we follow in this direction and we don't get great results right
away? What if we trust God and good things don't happen? What
if we lead people in a direction we believe to be God-inspired,
and they won't follow? This kind of leadership is scary and anxi-
ety-producing because it has a real potential for failure. Why?
Because this way of leadership depends upon seeking God's
path, a path that may not be completely clear to us, and not upon
following the safe paths of human convention. For example, as
pastor of Calvin Presbyterian Church, I've been trying my best

to lead us in God's direction by encouraging other lay leaders to make discernment of God's will a passion. In a practical sense, this approach sometimes means that I don't exactly know where we are going, but I try to keep people calm, faithful, and ready for opportunities that God presents to us. I've learned that becoming open to God means following wherever God leads even if the way is obscured, for as the Bible shows, God often calls leaders to lead people to promised lands that can't be seen until the very end.

Imagine that you were one of the original apostles. I can imagine that they wanted nothing more than to live out safe lives cloistered in Jerusalem, tending to the already converted. Instead, according to Christian tradition, God led all of them out of Jerusalem to places like Damascus, Antioch, Ephesus, Rome, Spain, Armenia, Persia, India, and Ethiopia. They were led to spread the gospel throughout the world, sometimes experiencing great success, and at other times being beaten, tortured, and imprisoned. All but John were killed violently because of their leadership. There is danger in following God, in being open to God: we might get sent to places of conflict, where the people don't necessarily want what we offer, where they make a habit of running off those carrying God's Word.

The danger entailed in being open to God as a leader is especially evident with some pastors. As a spiritual director I've worked with many pastors in conflicted situations. I used to believe that if we were ministering and leading properly, the congregations we serve should always be places of peace and harmony. What I've learned is that there are some congregations that even the best pastor cannot turn around. Yet God still calls leaders to these churches. And sometimes we are called to be leaders in congregations that don't want our leadership. If we are open to God's guidance, we have to be open to the possibility of being sent to these churches. We have to consider the possibility that our being in a place of conflict doesn't mean that God made a mistake. As the apostles showed, God sends humble leaders to places that may be painful and troubled. But we're still called. And just like the apostles, we're called to lead these churches, even if we don't know what the destination will be.

There may be real danger in becoming radically open to God, but there is also great freedom. The freedom comes in the ability to be creative. What I mean is that the more we lead churches to become what they have always been, the more we lead the church to do what it has always done. Humble leaders discover that they have the freedom to choose alternatives, to choose to do ministry in their congregations in ways that are creative and unique to their churches.

Radical openness to God, with the resulting freedom that arises from it, is what Gandhi experienced during his salt march. He was humble, prayerful, faithful, hopeful, and willing to do whatever God wanted. And as a result, God led him to an insight that attacking the British salt industry by creating a symbol of defiance—picking up salt from the ocean and declaring that he had manufactured salt—would eventually bring the British to their knees. And this is what happened.

The more we lead in a spirit of openness to God, the more God increases our freedom of choice by offering creative alternatives to what we had already been doing. We become freed from convention. We become more creative, seeing more possibilities. And we are able to help others see these possibilities, too. I've discovered how creativity leads to seeing possibilities in my own parish, Calvin Presbyterian Church. We've discovered that as we try to create worship grounded in what we sense God is calling us to do rather than in what the church has always done, we become more creative. At the same time, we become more sensitive to the needs of both those in our church and those potentially interested in our church. We are open to finding ways to reach out to both groups in worship. And we become more sensitive to different generations, finding ways to reach out to all of them rather than targeting just one, whether it is the youngest or oldest. Numerous worship wars are being fought today between Christians of different generations, all trying to push their own style of worship, especially when it comes to music. Some are traditionalists who believe that only music written prior to the 20th century can be sacred. Others believe that only praise music written after 1985 is suitable. Then there are those in between, trying to blend them all together. In our congregation, we attempt to integrate different elements into worship with one intent: seeking what God is calling us to do so that our worship can help people encounter Christ. As much as possible, our worship team—pastors, music directors, musicians, and choir—tries to be open to what we sense is right for us. We don't follow a formula. Instead, we follow our hearts in trying to create an experience that integrates all sorts of different elements.

For instance, a few years ago, we realized that the printed calls to worship featuring leader/congregation responses seemed stilted and artificial. It's sad to hear a congregation read without any emotion, as many congregations do, "We worship you today in joy!" These calls may be part of our Presbyterian tradition, but they didn't seem to open people to God in worship effectively. So we sensed a need to open our worship in a way that quieted people and opened them to God's presence. Our solution was to center people with a chant, offer them a short time for quiet prayer, and bless them with a prayer asking God to open them to God's presence. The effect was to create a more centered opening to worship.

When we become more open to God as leaders, we are freed to find creative ways to lead people more fruitfully to God. Humble leaders try to ground their leadership in openness to God, aware of how easy it is to close ourselves to God and to lead out of fear, willfulness, cynicism, selfishness, pride, and a sense of our own power. Leading from radical openness allows us to lead by following God's lead. And this way makes all the difference between leading a congregation to regard God as an idea or thought, and leading a congregation to a spiritual place where God is encountered and experienced.

WHAT IS HUMBLE LEADERSHIP?

It is difficult to be a humble leader today because we live in times in which power seems to mean everything. I'm not sure there was ever a time when power didn't mean everything. What's different today is that we live in a complex society with many more opportunities for people to become leaders. A hundred years ago, the majority of the population was employed as laborers who had little opportunity or need to be leaders. Leadership positions were held by very few at the top of steeply hierarchical organizations. Today in our culture more people than ever have some sort of leadership role, whether as teachers, managers, supervisors, vice-presidents, presidents, CEOs, CFOs, politicians, or even pastors. As hard as it is to find competent leaders, humble leaders can be even harder to find.

Humble leaders can be found, though, even in organizations in which achieving ambitions and wielding power seem to be obsessions. Jim Collins, a business researcher, wrote a groundbreaking book, *Good to Great,* based on his research into what makes some companies merely good and some truly great. He defines a great company as one that makes the leap from getting reasonably good results to getting truly great results, as measured by certain earnings and value statistics, and then sustains those results for at least 15 years.[5] In his research he found that one of the strongest factors in making a company great, an element that surprised Collins and the other researchers, was that the presidents and CEOs of the truly great companies were humble leaders. As Collins says, "We were surprised, shocked really, to discover the type of leadership required for turning a good company into a great one. Compared to high-profile leaders with big personalities who make headlines and become celebrities, the good-to-great leaders seem to have come from Mars. Self-effacing, quiet, reserved, even shy—these leaders are a paradoxical blend of personal humility and professional will."[6]

It's not just corporate cultures that respond to humble leadership. So do churches. Again, if we confuse humility with weakness, and then offer weak leadership, our churches will falter. But if our leaders have humility and a deep openness to God, a conviction that churches are called to follow God, a willingness to be weak so that God's grace and power can flow through us, and a resolute readiness to move people lovingly and compassionately in God's direction, amazing things can happen.

So what is humble leadership? Simply put, humble leadership is the willingness to lead others to follow Christ by being radically open to God's guidance and grace. It is a willingness to put aside fear, willfulness, pride, cynicism, a need for false clarity and certainty, as well as selfish desires and a need to wield our own power. Humble leaders put them aside by becoming aware of these self-focused, closed-off attributes. They are aware that these "closed to God" attributes arise out of the animal, created nature, a nature that even the must humble of us grapple with our whole lives. Humble leaders recognize that they overcome these attributes by becoming open to God's Spirit. Similarly, because they are rooted in openness, these leaders become more other- and God-focused. Finally, they become willing to lead others to the Spirit so that together in openness to God's Spirit the whole congregation can be led to seek and do God's will in everything. Fundamental to being aware of self, becoming other- and God-focused, and following the Spirit is the formation of a strong sense of faith, willingness, prayerfulness, and hopefulness, as well as the embrace of ambiguity, uncertainty, and mystery. To be a humble leader means to say to God, "I'm yours, no matter where you call me to go, what you call me to do, and how you call me to be. I will seek your will and way as I lead others to do the same."

2

Self-Aware Leadership

⊷ ≡✦≡ ⊷

[Jesus] also told this parable to some who trusted in themselves that they were righteous and regarded others with contempt: "Two men went up to the temple to pray, one a Pharisee and the other a tax collector. The Pharisee, standing by himself, was praying thus, 'God, I thank you that I am not like other people: thieves, rogues, adulterers, or even like this tax collector. I fast twice a week; I give a tenth of all my income.' But the tax collector, standing far off, would not even look up to heaven, but was beating his breast and saying, 'God, be merciful to me, a sinner!' I tell you, this man went down to his home justified rather than the other; for all who exalt themselves will be humbled, but all who humble themselves will be exalted."

Luke 18:9–14

WHY WAS IT THAT THE PHARISEE COULDN'T EMBRACE THE WAY OF humility? What allowed the tax collector to welcome it? The Pharisee, who was obviously a leader, was on a path that led away from God, even though he was deemed the righteous one by all but Christ. Meanwhile, the tax collector was on a path that led directly to God, although his vocation caused the Jews of his time to deem him unrighteous. Many think that the tax collector in question might have been the disciple Matthew, who became a great leader among the early Christians. What allowed him to humble himself when the more outwardly righteous Pharisee couldn't?

A central flaw afflicts all leaders, whether poor, mediocre, good, or great. It cannot be avoided, and it eventually brings down all leaders. What is this central flaw? It's the unexamined

29

pride that all leaders have. There comes a point at which leadership breaks down because of our success as leaders.

Good leadership requires confidence—the ability to believe in ourselves when others question and doubt our judgment, motivations, and vision. Confidence is essential, but when we begin to experience success, confidence eventually turns into pride and arrogance. Why? Because past success makes us careless, causing us to forget about the small things we did that led to success. It especially causes us to ignore the essential core of leadership: relationships. The more successful we get at anything—vocationally, athletically, or even religiously—the easier it is to forget how important relationships are. As we become successful, we fall prey to believing our own myth that the world revolves around us. As a result, we start seeing the people in our lives mainly in terms of how they are either assisting or impeding our success. Success in anything can lead to arrogance.

What lies at the core of this arrogance? Ignorance—ignorance of our motivations, our pride, and our pitfalls. Self-ignorance always feeds arrogance. Examples of how self-ignorance leads to arrogance abound in American culture, but nowhere more plainly than in the fates of many of our presidents.

For youth growing up in the United States, the most influential leader, especially in modeling leadership, is always our nation's president. We try to imitate their successes and overcome their faults. For example, President John F. Kennedy has profoundly affected many of those in the baby-boom generation. He appealed to younger people in a way that few earlier presidents could. He had an optimistic vision for the country, a nation still trying to rebuild its economy 15 years after the end of World War II. He had a vision of America the generous, an America of servants who serve those struggling with oppression and social stagnation. He started the Peace Corps to reach out to the impoverished worldwide. He initiated the Berlin airlift to bring food and supplies to the free people of Berlin who were cut off from the world by communist East Germany. When Kennedy increased the military presence in Vietnam, most people believed that this intervention would bring democracy and freedom to the people of South Vietnam. Kennedy offered a generation the hope that if we worked together, we could change the world. This hope was echoed in his famous inauguration speech: "Ask not what your country can do for you; ask what you can do for your country."

You can see the impact of Kennedyesque optimism in the boom of Christian megachurches. Mostly started by older boomers, they tend to be optimistic places. Even those that preach God's judgment against non-Christians have found a way to articulate their message in a positive, upbeat way, emphasizing the ultimate and assured salvation of those who worship with them. Boomer leaders generally are optimistic and buoyant, but what they fail to see in their brimming confidence is the Bay of Pigs. In the Bay of Pigs incident, the Central Intelligence Agency tried to overthrow the newly formed, Fidel Castro–led communist government of Cuba by using trained Cuban expatriates. This secret force landed in Cuba's "Bay of Pigs." The plot failed miserably for many reasons, but few are more glaring than the fact that the Kennedy administration, the CIA, and the U.S. military had all become overconfident and arrogant. They had become enraptured with their past successes (and with U.S. overthrows of governments in Iran in 1953 and Guatemala in 1954) and their overoptimistic vision of spreading freedom and democracy throughout the world. In the process they forgot about planning, training, and execution. They had become ignorant of what had carried them so far, and their ignorance fed their arrogance.

While Kennedy was a beacon to many older boomers, those of us who have come later have a darker presidential legacy. I'm in a "cusp" generation. Technically I am a boomer, but since I was born at the tail end of that generation, I share much in common with generation-Xers. In contrast to boomers, gen-Xers are often more cynical and skeptical of authority and of what can be accomplished by government or any kind of institution. Much of their cynicism is rooted in their presidential legacies: two monumental cases of presidential ignorance that led to arrogance.

The first was the presidency of Richard M. Nixon. Nixon was a contradiction: how could a man with so much talent and insight have been brought down by such stupidity as the Watergate break-in? The answer is that he created a paranoid climate that gave rise to the break-in, and then he employed an incredibly inept cover-up. There was no need for a break-in or cover-up. He was about to defeat Senator George McGovern in a landslide victory in the 1972 election. Ultimately his self-ignorance led to arrogance, his arrogance led to his disgrace, and his disgrace led to his resignation in the face of possible impeachment.

Despite his faults (and they were great), Nixon was a good leader. He did things that others before him couldn't do. He created the era of détente, in which the U. S. and the Soviet Union thawed relations and began to cooperate on certain ventures. He opened relationships with communist China after repeated failures by previous presidents. Still, Nixon was a deeply paranoid man. He saw enemies everywhere. He created a secret "enemies list" (it was a point of pride afterward for many Washington insiders, news reporters, and Democrats to boast that they were on Nixon's secret enemies list). Nixon was an extremely talented leader, but he was ignorant of his major flaw, and as a result, his administration came crashing down. The eventual failure of his leadership had an impact on later boomers and early gen-Xers by making us much more cynical about politics and politicians.

The second case of ignorance leading to arrogance was the presidency of William Jefferson Clinton—as the youngest members of generation X were moving into adulthood. Bill Clinton may be one of the most talented presidents this country has ever had. He had an intuitive understanding of politics. How else could he have snatched victory from the jaws of defeat so often? He weathered all sorts of crises throughout his political career, and it is a testament to his great political skill and leadership that he escaped most of these unscathed. That is, until he had one affair too many and then lied about it to the American public. The public would likely have forgiven his affair (they had done so with presidents and politicians in the past), but not his lying.

Clinton understood that good leadership is personal and relational, and he had the ability to make everyday people, and especially those with influence, feel as though they were his best friends. Still, he had a major flaw. He was ignorant of his sexual obsessions. His great ability to forge relationships was also his tragic weakness, as he obsessively pursued not only political relationships but sexual ones as well. Again, a potentially great leader was brought down by willful ignorance leading to arrogance.

What brings down so many leaders, no matter what their skill, is ignorance of their darker sides. This is especially true of congregational leadership. Too often congregational leaders use theological/biblical sophistication to hide from themselves their true natures. For example, they may wield authority manipulatively and justify it by claiming that they have a special relationship with God. They may use their ordained role to excuse their behavior, never taking the time for self-reflection and asking what motivates them to manipulate. The fact that religious leaders can add a seemingly divine dimension to their authority allows them to use this dimension to hide from themselves.

What impedes too many leaders, both religious and secular, is not their inability to lead so much as the fact that their darker side keeps undermining their leadership. They disregard the desires and urges that lurk in their depths and as a result end up making poor decisions that keep them from being effective. This darker side can be obscured by psychological and spiritual barriers. We all share spiritual blindness and psychological personality traits that have the power to impede our leadership, despite our spiritual depth and psychological maturity.

So how does a humble leader overcome these spiritual and psychological barriers? By trying his or her best to become self-aware spiritually and psychologically. Humble leaders are always self-aware leaders. They are self-critiquing leaders who are aware that they are ignorant. As a result of becoming self-aware, they make changes to their lives that improve the quality of their life and leadership. Because they are aware of the potential for their own self-destruction, they are willing to do what is necessary to overcome their darker motivations and to diminish their potential to abuse their leadership.

The following pages, then, will offer starting points for you to become more self-aware spiritually and psychologically.

Obviously we cannot cover this material in any real depth in one chapter, but what this chapter offers is some insight on where to start the process of becoming self-aware.

SPIRITUAL PITFALLS

Being a leader—congregational, political, corporate, or organizational—is a calling. It is a calling despite our society's tendency to split the world into secular and sacred realms and therefore to see God as acting in the religious realm but not in the marketplace. With God there is no secular/sacred split. The calling to be a leader is sacred in every realm. God calls people to become leaders and is ready to guide, support, and bless those who are open to Christ's presence in their leadership. Unfortunately, too few leaders recognize God's voice or take the Spirit's tangible presence seriously, especially in the so-called secular realm, and so their leadership never quite reaches its potential.

The basic problem, as I mentioned in my book *Becoming a Blessed Church*,[1] is that it is easy to functionalize life by ignoring the life's spiritual dimension. As a result, many leaders cut off the spiritual and lose all ability to invigorate their leadership with spiritual vibrancy. It's ironic that those charged with being spiritual leaders would ignore the spiritual. The lack of spiritual awareness is an unseen problem in secular leadership, too, but that's a topic for another book. Thus, the first spiritual pitfall we have to be aware of is the tendency of pastoral and spiritual leaders to follow secular models of leadership in the life of the church by *failing to integrate the spiritual and the functional*.

A friend of mine, a member of Calvin Presbyterian Church, has shown me how a person can lead in a secular field without giving up a sense of spiritual vitality and awareness. He is the president of a large, international corporation. Several years ago he shared with me his personal mission statement. It was a series of assertions declaring his personal, family, career, and corporate goals. The statement was similar to that of many people working in the corporate world, except that at the center of the statement was this goal: "Having a personal relationship with Christ, trusting him to guide me in my life's decisions." Placing Christ in the center is not what you would expect of someone leading a large secular company.

When I asked, he said that he had developed the mission statement during a difficult period in which he had drifted from serving Christ to serving only himself. He wrote it after a period of intense vocational, psychological, and spiritual self-reflection when it dawned on him that even though his work was secular, it was also his way of serving Christ.

Placing Christ at the center of his leadership has led him to discover the power that prayer and the Holy Spirit can have on his work. Many times he has told me stories about struggling to get a department or board on target in a meeting or of wrestling with the need to put a presentation together. In frustration and confusion he would pray, giving it to God. Afterward, amazing things would happen. A contentious meeting would suddenly turn harmonious, or an idea would crystallize all the elements of a presentation. He discovered something that humble leaders discover: that God wants us to do well as leaders, and putting Christ at the center of what we do opens a conduit for God's blessings, blessings that help us do well.

Unfortunately, too many pastors, like their secular counterparts, forget God in their leadership. Oh, they know that they are serving Christ, but few pastors really make praying and seeking Christ's will central to their leadership. This is especially true in the mainline church. While most mainline pastors originally went to seminary because they prayerfully sensed the call of Christ and then prayed their way through seminary as they prepared to serve their calling as pastors, too many came under the sway of the functionality of academic seminary study. Thus, too many have learned a functional style of leadership that is bereft of God. In effect, many pastors lead churches but lack that same prayerful passion with which they entered seminary. Unlike my friend who prays his way through his work as the head of a large, multinational corporation, these pastors do their work as though God were a distant ideal.

Too many pastors fail to integrate the spiritual into the functional by treating their churches like business organizations, emptying their congregations of their spiritual vibrancy. Their churches become places that talk *about* God, without actually connecting people *with* God. My previous book, *Becoming a Blessed Church,* deals more extensively with this topic. Suffice it to say that for many mainline pastors, functionality is the primary spiritual problem from which all others emanate.

Other spiritual pitfalls lie obscured in pastoral leaders' paths. One of the most dangerous is the result of good things gone bad—as when our spiritual strengths become weaknesses, or our spiritual gifts become burdens. Spiritual gifts, especially leadership gifts, may come from the Holy Spirit, but ironically they can drag us down. Many of the Christian mystics recognized how even gifts from God can become burdens. They recognized that God gave them gifts to accomplish their callings but that darker forces were always ready to corrupt these gifts. They recognized that over time we are all tempted to fall into the second spiritual pitfall: *worshiping the gift, not the giver.*

For example, Teresa of Avila, a gifted mystic and spiritual leader who reformed the Carmelite order in the 16th century, prayed that God would refrain from giving her any more gifts or consolations. The reason? She realized that the success derived from her gifts was causing her to focus more on the gifts than on God, to worship grace and not the *source* of grace. Her success was causing her to lose sight of God. As a humble and self-aware leader, she recognized the danger of God's gifts. As she says, "However many consolations and pledges of love the Lord may give you, therefore, you must never be so sure of yourselves that you cease to be afraid of falling back again, and you must keep yourselves from occasions of sin."[2] In other words, to be a humble leader means to be aware of how our success can trap us by focusing our devotion upon our gifts rather than on God, who gave us those gifts.

The tendency to worship the gift, not the giver, afflicts all pastoral leaders. All the best pastoral leaders sense that they are on some sort of "mission from God." They feel as though God has personally given them a mission to lead their congregation to become a thriving church. They feel this calling in their bones, and they are right to call it a divine mission, for it is. The best pastoral leaders sense that their divine work is to create a congregation where God is present and experienced. I believe that I am on a "mission from God." Whether it is through my ministry, leadership, preaching, teaching, writing, counseling, or work as a spiritual director, I am clear that my mission is to lead people to an experience of the Trinity—to experience God's purpose, presence, and power in their lives.

It is this sense of mission that allows pastors to persevere through exhaustion, confusion, criticism, long hours, low pay, and life in a fishbowl. We believe that we are on a mission, and we are willing to undergo and do almost anything to see that mission fulfilled. Our spiritual gifts are the tools God gives us to accomplish our mission, yet over time we can confuse our gifts with the giver by thinking that these gifts are enough. We become overdependent on them. We forget that God can do more than we can accomplish by ourselves. Becoming dependent on our abilities alone, we plunge into despair when our gifts fail us in a crisis. We can't understand why we aren't receiving more help from God. Our dependence on gifts has caused us to see ourselves as somehow providentially destined, by tightening the grip of arrogance and pride over our lives and ministry. Eventually, if we become a smashing success by the world's standards, we mistake our talents, which are a gift, with the giver, thinking that possessing this "gift" somehow makes us closer to God, the giver.

We overcome this pitfall by always remembering that even though we are on a mission, we are on God's mission, and we are bit players in God's great drama. We are given only small glimpses of that expansive vision and a small time to accomplish our part in God's plan. In the overall scheme of things our mission is always infinitesimal in relation to everything God is doing in the universe. And so we need to maintain a sense of humility, being thankful for what God has given us but not forgetting that it all comes from God.

A third pitfall, one that is related to the confusion of the gift with the giver, is *overidentifying our thoughts with God's thoughts*. This mistake is especially a problem for successful pastors who have experienced growth and blessings in their ministry, as well as for pastors who see themselves as part of the prophetic tradition in ministry. In both cases hubris easily creeps into ministry. In the first case it happens because pastors see what they have done, and like David at the height of his reign, they believe they can do no wrong. They see God's hand blessing so much of what they've done that they feel as though they are in a spiritual "zone," much like the "zone" athletes experience when it seems that they can do no wrong. For example, a pitcher "in the zone" seems to throw only strikes. A quarterback in the zone seems to throw only completions. A goalie in the zone seems to save every ball or puck. Pastors and spiritual leaders can also feel as though they are in the zone, but when this happens, it often creates the context for hubris.

For instance, I've noticed that there seem to be two kinds of pastors who end up having affairs. Some affairs call on us to have pity and compassion for the clergy, even if it also means they should leave ministry until they address the root problems that led to their misconduct. These are pastors who feel alone and isolated. They are not arrogant. They are lonely and lost. This does not mean that they shouldn't be held accountable. They have violated a trust, and they have misused the influence and authority of their position to engage in a relationship that takes advantage of another's vulnerability. To say that some pastoral affairs begin in loneliness on the part of pastors does not condone the behavior. It's simply a recognition that pastors can end up having affairs for a variety of reasons that come together to create a stew of personal struggles marinated in unrealistic expectations. Their marriages suffer, but their anxiety is such that they fear that they cannot tell anyone, even their spouse, how confused and lonely they feel. They feel consumed by the pressures of a ministry that requires too many skills that few clergy possess in full: preaching, teaching, visiting, counseling, evangelism, mission, organization, management, and personal piety. They are plagued by members' expectations that they be spiritually mature, mentally tough, and physically healthy, all while having strong marriages and families, even though they are expected to be constantly available to those in need, 24/7. And to top it off, they are expected to accept criticism without ever taking it personally. Fearing what others, especially parishioners, might think, they hide their despair.

Thus, the affairs become a small ray of hope and pleasure amid a darkly swirling existence. These pastors are to be sympathized with and helped, even if they should also be ushered quickly and resolutely out of ordained ministry. Wanting to sympathize and help them should not be confused with tolerating what they have done.

The other group, though, become destructive precisely because of their success, pride, and arrogance. They engage in affairs because they see themselves as invulnerable, even to God, believing that their thoughts are God's thoughts, their desires are God's desires for them. A pastor of this region recently left ordained ministry because of an affair that has been destructive to his family, his paramour's family, the church, and many other lives influenced by the church. The church has tried to keep this affair quiet because of the damage it has done, offering the pastor a severance package that allows him to retire early with medical and pension benefits. Still, the misconduct has divided much of the congregation, especially since he has refused to end the illicit relationship. It is apparent that his tremendous success as a pastor has led him to see his affair as a reward from God, just as David believed that Bathsheba was his reward for his service to God. His hubris has warped his judgment, convincing him that anything he does must be what God wants, because he and God are so close in thought. Surely his success has demonstrated that, right? *Wrong.*

In the past, other, more famous figures have similarly wreaked havoc through sexual misconduct. The 1980s televangelist Jim Bakker is an example. He seemed to have initiated his affair with Jessica Hahn precisely because he believed that his success merited a reward—and she was his reward. He confused his own lust with God's personal call to him. Often people who enjoy great success are able to persuade themselves that their more base motivations are somehow really inspirations from God. Perhaps this tendency explains why so many charismatic cult leaders engage in sexual manipulation: they confuse their lusts with God's guidance, when in fact they lust for both sex and power.

This is one example of how pitfalls can appear when we overidentify our thoughts with God's thoughts, our desires with

God's desires, but in reality this overidentification usually takes place in more subtle ways. It takes place as pastors and other spiritual leaders, convinced that whatever they want must be what God wants, manipulate the people of the church. They can manipulate by subtly or overtly suggesting to others that because they have gone to seminary, have spent so much time in prayer, have had great past success, or hold the position of pastor, they inherently know more of what God wants than others. While that may be true to some extent, when we become believers in our own holiness we reduce our ability to discern what God wants.

C. S. Lewis gives a wonderful example of how easy it is for our spiritual successes, especially our successes in becoming humble, to subtly convince us of our perfection—that we are what God wants. In his great book *The Screwtape Letters*, Lewis explores this pitfall through the fictional correspondence between demons trying to keep a man (whom the demons call "the patient") from growing spiritually. The demon, Screwtape, writes to his protege, Wormwood, saying, "Your patient has become humble; have you drawn his attention to the fact? All virtues are less formidable to us once the man is aware that he has them, but this is especially true of humility. Catch him at the moment when he is really poor in spirit and smuggle into his mind the gratifying reflection, 'By jove! I'm being humble,' and almost immediately pride—pride at his own humility—will appear."[3] Lewis warns us that pride is tricky, and that we can easily fool ourselves by taking pride in our attempts to become humble.

The antidote to overidentifying with God lies in always questioning our motives, perceptions, and beliefs. Ultimately the question we need to ask about our discernments or decisions in any leadership situation is, "Is this from God, from me, or from something else?" The more we are willing to ask and honestly answer this question, the more our leadership will become naturally humble.

Many more spiritual pitfalls will be explored as this book progresses, but for now, I want to explore important psychological pitfalls that afflict many spiritual leaders and lead to a lack of humility, for often it's the psychological pitfalls that lead to deeper spiritual pitfalls.

PSYCHOLOGICAL PITFALLS

Every human being is unique not only because of her spiritual gifts, but because each person is a distinct amalgamation of instinct, conditioning, experiences, and perceptions. Each of us brings a certain psychological constitution to our lives that is the result of our biogenetic packaging, social learning, and lived experiences. All of these factors create our *personality*—the blend of personal psychological characteristics that makes us distinct. Psychologists have studied personality and personality traits for more than a hundred years, and while they are able to distinguish certain personality profiles that are particularly unhealthy, they struggle to tell us what personality traits and profiles are typical of healthy people. Thus, they have not been able to distinguish a definitive personality profile for healthy and effective leaders.

What psychology has been able to do, and do effectively, is to point out personality *disorders* that interfere with normal and healthy human living. Thus, it has given us a wonderful gift by pointing out particular psychological pitfalls that can interfere with healthy life, as well as with effective, humble leadership.

My focus in this section will be to mine clinically tested observations of modern psychology and psychiatry. In particular I want to focus on specific personality traits that can progress to become *personality disorders.* A personality disorder is a collection of strong, negative personality traits that together create a self-destructive and self-defeating pattern of behavior. In simpler terms, people with personality disorders live chaotic lives strewn with unhealthy, strained, or broken relationships. As a result of this chaos, they are unable to bring stability and wholeness to their lives. Simply put, they drive other people crazy. Through my own training and experience as a counselor, I've noticed that leaders with personality traits associated with these disorders often struggle, because their leadership is undermined by their personal psychological pitfalls.

It's a shame that more pastoral and spiritual leaders, and especially those who train them, are not more aware of these personality disorders, because pastors and members with their traits generally are at the center of most church conflicts. Many pastors, spiritual directors, and religious people are aware of personality inventories such as the Myers-Briggs Type Indicator and the Enneagram, which are both good assessments to help us understand our perceptions or ways of interacting with others. Still, even having studied both thoroughly, I find the personality disorders I learned about as a therapist most valuable in helping me understand the psychological pitfalls of leadership, as well as how to deal with those in our churches who typically suffer from these kinds of personality traits and disorders. What's the difference between a trait and a disorder? A personality disorder is a dysfunctional set of personality characteristics that create chaos in our lives. When I say that we exhibit *traits* of a personality disorder, I mean that although we may not have a full-blown disorder, we do seem to exhibit some personality qualities that are related to those of a disorder and that may periodically create the same kind of dysfunction. Most spiritual leaders won't have a disorder, but they will have traits related to disorders. And under stress their reactions to crises and problems can exhibit traits of a disorder.

Eleven personality disorders are identified by the *Diagnostic and Statistical Manual of Mental Disorders-IV-TR,* which is the preeminent resource of diagnostic standards for those working in the mental health field.[4] The sheer dysfunctional nature of most of these personality disorders, such as schizoid, paranoid, schizotypal, and antisocial personality disorders, keeps those suffering with them from becoming pastoral or even lay leaders. As a result, I won't focus on all 11 personality disorders but only on four types exhibited by many pastoral leaders. In the process of discussing these disorders, I will also spend a little time discussing how healthy leaders can deal with members suffering from these disorders and their traits. The following descriptions grow out of my observations as a pastor, spiritual director, and therapist. I am unaware of empirical data to support my observations, but I do believe these observations merit future research.

HISTRIONIC PERSONALITIES

Have you ever met a pastor who is dynamic, charismatic, funny, and engaging, while also being totally disorganized, harried, and conflicted? He or she is probably a person bearing personality traits related to *histrionic personality disorder.* Ministry can be especially attractive to histrionics, because they crave the spotlight, and are very good at grabbing it. What's especially engaging about them is that they are attractive to others physically and sexually, although they might not be actually beautiful. They have an innate ability to attract people.

Many of those familiar with this disorder believe that the movie and music businesses are dominated by histrionics. Who else but histrionics can offer such powerful emotion on demand? You see, histrionics are emotional dynamos, quick to laugh and cry. In essence, they have Ph.D.s in emotion and are exciting to be around because of their ability to generate amusement, arousal, and laughter. But this ability has a downside. With their ability to generate excitement comes an ability to create melodrama. Histrionics seem to be in some sort of perpetual crisis, whether personal, marital, familial, or communal. And conflict always reigns. Histrionics often portray themselves as victims of others' insensitivity or cruelty, and they try to get others to rescue them, even though the truth is that they really can't be rescued, because they are rarely in a true crisis. They manufacture crises as a way of keeping rescuers in constant orbit around them.

Pastors or other leaders with healthy histrionic traits can be dynamic presences who lead people to heights and depths of emotion. When preaching, they can lead people to laugh, cry, and feel inspired. When they are in performance mode, especially when leading worship, they are charismatic. When visiting or doing pastoral work with parishioners, histrionics can make them feel as though they are the most important people in the world. Histrionics also seem truly, deeply to understand the congregants' pain and struggles. As group leaders, they can create emotionally deep and cohesive groups while also bringing a great sense of humor and levity. The most prominent histrionic pastoral leader of the early 20th century was Aimee Semple McPherson, the Pentecostal preacher who dominated the radio and the newspapers during the 1920s with her theatrical brand of religion.

Problems arise with those who are unhealthy histrionics. They may be able to do everything mentioned above, but behind the scenes they become temperamental, often throwing fits and expecting others to clean up their messes. They say nasty things to others, expecting to be forgiven, but then they themselves rarely forgive those who have slighted them. They have the uncanny ability to create conflict where otherwise there is none, and then to walk away from conflict as though nothing had happened. This behavior is especially common with those who suffer from *borderline personality disorder.*

Borderline personality disorder is closely associated with histrionic personality disorder and can easily be confused with it. Borderlines take the emotional instability of histrionic personality disorder and amplify it by seemingly turning everything into a black-and-white, good-and-evil struggle. Borderlines tend to see people and events in absolutes: those who are with them and support them (who are good) and those who are against them (their enemies). In reality the two disorders are distinct, but in my experience they are so close in character that the differences often seem only a matter of degree. Borderlines exhibit all the characteristics of histrionics but add a higher degree of anger, paranoia, and overidealization of self, along with either an over- or undervaluing of others. The main difference between the two is that the histrionic reacts to the world emotionally, feeling her way through life, and often getting lost in the emotional chaos she feels around her. The borderline feels the same chaos, but tries to get control over it by manipulating other people's emotions. For instance, a histrionic might break down into tears when a problem arises, feeling overwhelmed and confused, and then shutting down saying that she can't handle it anymore. The borderline comes out swinging in the midst of a problem, trying to figure out who is at fault, and trying to get everyone stirred up about the injustice of it all.

I saw a clear example of a histrionic/borderline personality in my ministry with a church elder who sowed conflict in her wake. She was such a dynamic presence that she seemed an obvious choice to become an elder. But when she took over the leadership of our Christian education committee, the committee quickly fell apart. She would generate ideas and then get angry when others didn't quickly volunteer to carry them out. The meetings she led were unstable, and soon the other members of the committee found reasons not to continue on the committee. One night, three months into her leadership, she called the previous chair of the committee on the telephone and chewed her out for 45 minutes, saying that if this woman had been her employee, she would have been fired for insubordination. She accused another member of the committee, one of the most deeply prayerful, loving, and spiritual members of the church, of making faces at her behind her back.

One night after a church board meeting, during a process to discern whether we needed to hire a part-time Christian education director, she went to town on me. I had solicited the opinion of a respected member of our church, who had worked in Christian education for more than 50 years, about the wisdom of our plan, and she had sent me a letter suggesting a different course of action. When I told the elder about the letter, she proceeded to blast me, saying that I really didn't care about the youth and children of our church, that I was undermining her, and that I was the problem. I was dumbfounded. Trying to remain calm, I simply repeated what the letter said, saying that it wasn't my opinion—that it was the opinion of someone else. I led her to my office and showed her the letter. She read it, looked at me, smiled, and said of the recommendation, "Oh, that's what I wanted in the first place." Then she turned and walked away, leaving me feeling as though I had just been the victim of a tornado.

Histrionic leaders can be tremendously gifted, but they can also be tremendously conflicted. So what do you do if you are a pastor or leader and suspect that you have these traits and tendencies? The first answer I would give anyone, especially one seeking to be a humble leader, is to seek the help of a counselor—not because the condition is hopeless, but because a good therapist can help someone with histrionic tendencies to stabilize and find ways to accentuate the positive qualities and become aware of the pitfalls of the negative traits. (I'll offer the same blanket suggestion for those with all of the following traits and disorders.) Pastoral and spiritual leaders with histrionic traits or disorder need to work on integrating the intellectual with the emotional, especially by trying to disengage from their emotions to seek a more objective view. Histrionics suffer from the tendency to see everything through an emotional lens, a lens that often leaves them feeling that they are the only ones with their own special emotional sensitivity. What they need to do is learn to assess situations intellectually, from a more detached, objective, self-effacing, and humble perspective. They need to begin to distrust their pure emotions and to integrate a more rational way of seeing. The goal is not for them to become unemotional but to become more objective, trying to see themselves and their ministries from a more humble, realistic, and (dare we say) God-oriented perspective.

Ultimately, if I know that I have histrionic tendencies, my goal should be humbly to recognize my anxieties, calm them, and try to detach. It helps to recognize that the fact that I emotionally perceive something to be true doesn't mean that it is. I need to be somewhat, but not entirely, skeptical of my emotions. I need first to assess a situation cognitively, which might mean asking someone I respect who seems to be objective. The more I practice detachment and seek objectivity, the more I develop the ability to deal with situations without creating drama.

From a spiritual perspective, the histrionic often benefits most from time spent in intellectual study of biblical, theological, devotional, and spiritual literature. This intellectual study brings about an integration of the mind and emotions by helping the histrionic recognize life from a more cognitive perspective. Time spent in contemplative prayer can also help histrionics by bringing a sense of calm and centeredness to their lives. Two spiritual exercises or approaches can also help. Keeping a journal helps histrionics, because it encourages them to sit down and reflect on their lives from a more detached perspective. Also, the Ignatian spiritual exercises and approach can help a histrionic gain a more balanced perspective on her or his spiritual path. An excellent resource on the Ignatian exercises is Thomas H. Green's book *Weeds Among the Wheat*.[5]

For a pastor dealing with a histrionic member, the most important skill is staying calm. Responding to a histrionic, and especially a borderline, with anger, indignation, or raised voice only exacerbates the situation. It adds fuel to the fire. Calmness and clarity defuse the situation. Histrionics, and especially borderlines, always try to pull us into the drama. By remaining calm and continually repeating our beliefs, perceptions, and stances, we try to help the histrionic snap out of the emotion. Conversely, histrionics may verbally blast us and then storm away. Sometimes that just happens. In their anger they can make us targets, trying their best to create conflict by encouraging others to take their side against us. Our best defense is calmness, honesty, and integrity in dealing with those caught up in the conflict. If we keep our responses healthy, the healthy leaders of the church will recognize the drama for what it is. What I've noticed with many pastors afflicted by histrionics and borderlines in their congregations is that their refusal to join in the drama causes the mildly unhealthy histrionics/borderlines to use the church as a safe environment in which to become healthier, and the unhealthy histrionics/borderlines to increase their attempts to bring division. But most unhealthy histrionics, finding no one to resonate with their drama, will eventually become frustrated and leave the congregation. Sad to say, that is almost always the best outcome for the church saddled with histrionics who refuse to become healthier.

NARCISSISTIC PERSONALITIES

The second personality disorder that commonly afflicts pastors and leaders is *narcissistic personality disorder.* You'll quickly recognize why ministry attracts those with narcissistic tendencies, traits, and disorders. As the name suggests, these are pastors and leaders who tend toward self-absorption, grandiosity, and a conviction of their own preeminence. Leadership attracts narcissists because it offers the potential for them to subjugate others to their will. On the positive side, healthy narcissists—those who are aware of their own self-absorption and are working on humility—lead well because they have a sense of confidence and trust that allows others to follow with assurance. Healthy narcissists can be good at leading large organizations both because of their inherent leadership abilities and because the size of the organization keeps them from having to engage in overly intimate relationships, thus hiding their self-righteous and arrogant tendencies.

Unfortunately, many religious leaders suffer from narcissistic tendencies and traits. Unhealthy narcissists tend to be consumed with amassing power and influence. They have a tremendous sense of self-importance about their ministries, sometimes believing that only they and their followers are saved. They often exaggerate their achievements and talents, believing that they are special, unique, and the center of the universe. Their sense of entitlement causes them to exploit others, seeing others only in terms of how they can assist or obstruct their ministry. For instance, some unhealthy narcissists see the members of their churches mainly as numbers, statistical units to measure their success. They try to assess what they have accomplished in terms of church size and worship participation. For the narcissist, only large churches matter, for they serve as monuments to their own greatness, not God's.

As you can imagine, unhealthy narcissists can be very successful. While unhealthy histrionic pastors are often weeded out because of the conflict surrounding them, unhealthy narcissists can become highly accomplished before their actions undo them. Narcissistic pastors who achieve success are often undone by the scandals they eventually engage in: affairs, embezzlements, abuse of others, addictions, or some other self-focused disgrace.

It's not only pastors who suffer from these narcissistic tendencies. Politics is filled with healthy and unhealthy narcissists, as are corporate boardrooms and local boards. Narcissists crave power, and so they seek power positions in society. I could point out prominent narcissists throughout our culture—in religious, political, or corporate life. But the truth is that I don't have to. Throw a dart at any religious, political, or corporate figure hogging media attention, and you will most likely hit a narcissist.

If we are aware of our narcissistic tendencies and decide to become humble leaders, we can become wonderful leaders, but the transition to humble leadership requires a clear awareness of our narcissistic tendencies. The narcissistic pastor must develop the ability to be self-accusatory and self-critical. Don't worry that becoming self-accusing and critical will lead to a loss of self-esteem. A narcissist will never let that happen. Self-accusation and criticism merely strip away narcissism. They don't lead to self-debasement.

Humility requires the narcissist always to assess himself humbly to determine whether his self-perceptions are merited or aggrandized. He must develop the ability to become weak, share power, and delegate authority. He must always remind himself that he is not, nor ever will be, the center of the universe (a particularly hard awareness for the narcissist). A narcissist who wants to become more humble is encouraged to spend time with others out of the spotlight. Mission trips to places where participants have no power or influence and must do simple tasks can be very helpful in showing the narcissist his place in the universe. Working with the poor or in ministries where success cannot be measured also humbles the narcissist. Unfortunately, the innate tendencies of narcissists can cause them to use mission work as proof of their personal sanctification and holiness. For example, I cringe every time I see a narcissistic pastor appearing before a camera in some third-world country, using images of the poor and starving in the background simultaneously to encourage people to give to his ministry and to demonstrate his own true righteousness. The message seems inescapable: "Look at me, look at me, look at me! I'm so great and humble because I care about the poor! Oh, and give to my ministry, and I'll send you a free Bible embossed with my name." Despite this possible abuse, working in mission can be a great and humbling tonic for the narcissist. Finally, the regular practice of honest confession, especially with another person, can humble and free a narcissist.

DEPENDENT PERSONALITY

This is an odd personality disorder to associate with leadership because it renders people unable to lead others effectively. Yet I have seen quite a few pastors and lay leaders afflicted with at least the traits of this disorder, if not the disorder itself. The disorder seems an uncharacteristic one for those in leadership roles because it would seem to bar a person from serving as an even mildly effective leader. But you can see evidence of this disorder in pastors and leaders who have little or no confidence in their abilities, are always seeking the guidance and direction of others, and end up being bullied by others.

People who struggle with dependent personality traits tend to be submissive and clingy, constantly and almost desperately needing the approval of others. They struggle to make independent decisions on even small matters and to accept full responsibility for their leadership. Their basic problem is that their lives are filled with fear, especially fear of disagreeing with and offending others. They struggle to initiate projects and to develop creative ideas. They will do almost anything to ingratiate themselves with others and to obtain their support and approval.

From my observation, most pastoral leaders who exhibit dependent personality traits are associate or assistant pastors or are solo pastors in very small congregations with fewer than 50 people attending worship weekly. These people have been traditionally called "neurotic," even though that term is no longer considered a valid psychological diagnosis or term. Often they are manipulated and exploited by others, and their lack of leadership can create the conditions for conflict as members try to fill the void. When dependents serve as associates, their lack of confidence and leadership ability can be masked by a strong senior pastor who gives steady guidance, support, and direction, allowing the associate to function as a task completer, seeking to appease and win the approval of the senior pastor who serves as a healthy father or mother figure. The real problem arises either when a dependent associate works with a narcissistic and manipulative senior pastor, or when the dependent is a solo pastor controlled by a narcissistically manipulative member. Under stress, dependents can become paralyzed by self-doubt and even self-loathing as they seek someone, anyone to take their load and deal with their problems. Dependents often choose a passive-aggressive route to deal with conflict, trying to be appealing and appeasing on the outside as they secretly gum up the works on the inside. This mode of operation allows them to plausibly deny their own failures while causing turmoil for others.

Finally, one of the most difficult aspects of dealing with dependents is that they tend to see themselves as victims—a trait
they share with histrionics. Dependents see themselves especially as victims of stronger, authoritarian figures. This characteristic
is part of their appeal to others. They are good at getting others
to see them as victims, too, and then setting about trying to alleviate their oppression. What makes their victimhood especially
perplexing is that they are often attracted to narcissists—a trait
that can make for dysfunctional relationships in which the dependent truly is victimized. Therefore, because they never make
the decision to take charge of their lives and change their oppres-
sive relationships, they remain victims despite the best efforts of
others to alleviate their suffering. While it is never right to blame
victims for their plight, sometimes dependents are victims and
yet are to blame for not taking steps to remove themselves from
the perpetual role of victim.

In my experience, pastors and lay leaders who have dependent personality disorder traits can be effective in several areas
of ministry. I have doubts that someone with a full-blown dependent personality disorder can be successful because his disorder
cripples his ability to do anything effectively other than the most
basic and clear-cut tasks. Yet those with the traits can excel in
certain areas.

For example, I worked years ago as a spiritual director with
a woman who seemed to exhibit strong dependent personality
disorder traits, and she was reasonably effective as a pastor. She
was the pastor of two small congregations. Her preaching was
relatively good although she didn't necessarily have a strong
presence in the pulpit. Her leadership was somewhat effective
even if it lacked creativity. She mostly led the congregation to do
those activities that small churches traditionally have done—activities that make them quaint, familiar places but that also tend
to inhibit growth. Still, she did excel in one area: pastoral care.
This is a woman whose dependent personality actually enhanced
her pastoral care. She wanted so much to be liked and loved that
when she visited people grappling with illness, brokenness, and
pain, her wanting to be loved enabled her to reach out to these
people and help them to feel loved. The result is that people paid

attention to her preaching and followed her leadership precisely because they felt that she loved them.

When she first went to her churches, she struggled because her dependent personality sometimes caused others to treat her as a sacrificial lamb, heaping their own brokenness onto her. They didn't always treat her well or with respect, but she had such a drive not only to please them but to please God that she worked overtime to get them to love her and to feel loved in return. And she succeeded. I don't want to portray her ministry as some sort of Nirvana. She still struggles to lead her small churches, but where she excels is in reaching out pastorally.

It's in this same sort of ministry that dependents can excel as associates or assistants. Often dependents, when they have a handle on their dependency, can be extremely effective in pastoral care. They have an innate ability to reach out to those who are struggling and to help them feel useful and worthwhile. This is especially true when their position is clearly defined and they have strong senior pastoral leadership supervising or guiding them. The biggest problem is that they can quickly and easily lose their sense of self-esteem. In fact, my suspicion is that the whole cult of self-esteem has arisen because of the prevalence of those with dependent personality traits in our culture. Psychologists, counselors, teachers, parents, and others have noticed these personality traits in adults and have determined that the lack of a nurturing, praising environment creates dependents. So they have emphasized the development of self-esteem in all people. The irony is that the cult of self-esteem has fed those with narcissistic tendencies and has created a culture filled with an overabundance of narcissists in the political, corporate, athletic, artistic, and entertainment fields.

So how does someone with dependent personality traits overcome them spiritually? This is a difficult question because growing spiritually requires a relatively healthy ego that can be self-critical but not self-debasing. The process of becoming humble requires letting go of ego. When we have no ego, we also have no basis upon which to become humble, for humility is the state of having voluntarily given up pride, arrogance, ego, and selfishness. Unfortunately, the dependent person can become so immersed in self-criticism, fear, a disregard of personal abilities and strengths, and low self-esteem that humility loses out to self-humiliation.

The secret, from a spiritual perspective, is to work on surrendering to God in a way that uses the dependency in a positive spiritual manner. The dependent needs to focus on seeking *only* God's approval, eschewing the pursuit of others' sanction. His prayer life needs to focus constantly on discerning God's will and then on developing the courage to stand by decisions based on discernment rather than kowtowing to stronger personalities around him. Becoming grounded only in God's approval is a very difficult thing for dependents to accomplish. Most dependents just don't have the internal strength to take a stand. The hard part is that in their prayer life it is relatively easy for them to make the mistake of assuming that the interpretation of God's will offered by another, stronger Christian is actually God's will. Time spent away from others in personal prayer can be helpful to them because it helps them to get away from stronger personalities and in the process to learn to trust their in their own inner guidance. Also, finding a good spiritual director who has the ability simultaneously to hold the dependent accountable while also praising him is crucial.

Despite the pitfalls of dependency in leadership, dependents do make great followers of healthy leaders, even if they sometimes have trouble following through on a project. Many church volunteers and workers have dependent personality traits. They love to do what strong, healthy pastors ask them to do. As a pastoral leader, though, I must always be cognizant of their fragility. I need to be willing, when they fail, to take the responsibility for their failure on my shoulders by telling them that I should have been more clear, or that I should have done more to help them. Getting angry at them for their failures, and even trying to hold them accountable in an authoritarian, critical way can be self-defeating if not handled tactfully. A dependent who feels scorned can be very good at gumming up the works passive-aggressively by intentionally not doing what he is supposed to do. Still, when handled in a caring and loving way, dependents can take the church a long way toward becoming a caring community.

OBSESSIVE-COMPULSIVE PERSONALITY

The final personality disorder we need to consider is *obsessive-compulsive personality disorder.* Don't confuse this with obsessive-compulsive disorder (OCD), which is a disorder resulting from a medical imbalance. Obsessive-compulsive *personality* disorder is less pervasive. Those with OCD typically cannot function in normal life without the aid of medication. Those with a personality disorder can, even if they drive others crazy in the process.

Those with obsessive-compulsive traits are obsessed with control and order. They believe that the secret to life is managing to get everything in order. They are perfectionists consumed with detail who become excessively focused on work and the need to accomplish and achieve. They also are overconcerned with morality, ethics, and values. They cannot delegate tasks, discard worn-out or worthless articles, share, or even gain a sense of perspective on what is balanced and what is extreme.

Many pastors and lay leaders struggle with obsessive-compulsive personality traits. The irony is that many of them, when they work in ministry, can be initially successful as they bring much-needed structure to churches. But over time their rigidity and lack of emotional resonance with others erodes what they have built up. They create structure, but their cold, controlling, and perfectionist style of leadership causes people eventually to disengage from the church.

In a church I was associated with many years ago before I became a pastor, I saw how overfocusing on structure can lead members to disengage. The church had been successful in its past, but when the pastor died, the congregation hired a new pastor who had obsessive-compulsive tendencies. Under his tutelage, the church became structurally clear, but it suffered relationally. What had allowed it to grow was the previous pastor's warmth and love. The new pastor tried to love the people of the church, but his obsessive-compulsive traits got in the way. Given a choice between visiting the members and doing the nitty-gritty organizational work of the church, he always opted for the organizational work. Trying to keep the church orderly, clean, and organized was a full-time job, and he was reluctant to delegate authority to others, lest they do a poor job of administering and accomplishing these tasks. He had his hand in everything and would not allow the members of the church to make decisions independent of him. He controlled the flow of information and the ministries. He stocked committees with people he chose, but no meeting could take place without him, and after discussions all eyes turned to him as he made all the decisions. Over the course of his time there, the church shrunk dramatically, losing almost 1,000 members.

Unfortunately, many large churches attract these kinds of pastors, because they come across as organizational people, and large churches tend to err on the side of thinking that organization is all that matters in the operation of a large church. However, over time overcontrolling leadership stifles creativity, initiative, and energy in members, causing people simply to give all ministry back to the pastor.

Actually, having obsessive-compulsive members can seem like a gift to pastors. Members with obsessive-compulsive traits tend to get things done, a reality that explains why so many churches stock their committees and even church boards with obsessive-compulsives. They are good at coordinating church dinners, clean-ups, clothing drives, and so much more. Narcissistic and even histrionic pastors find them easy to manipulate, because of their perfectionistic and moralistic tendencies. Simply put, obsessive-compulsives want to please God, so it is easy to use their guilt to keep them working, even to the point of exhaustion. The downside is that their obsessive-compulsive nature can cause them difficulty in working with others. They want to do everything, so while they may gather together a large group to help them in a church venture, their unwillingness to delegate means that volunteers will always stand idle, watching the obsessive-compulsive do all the work. And then the obsessive-compulsive becomes angry at the unwillingness of the others to do any work. It's a conundrum. The volunteers don't help because the obsessive-compulsive won't let them, but then the obsessive-compulsive becomes furious at them for not helping.

Ironically, obsessive-compulsives create their own messes because of their obsession with eradicating disorder.

So, if we suspect that we have obsessive-compulsive personality traits, what do we do spiritually? This is a difficult question to answer because the answer lies in doing precisely what obsessive-compulsives cannot do: relinquish control. Their main goal must be to do something that sounds trite: let go and let God. They have to practice the spiritual discipline of relinquishing control, order, and results. This is an almost impossible task for the obsessive-compulsive personality. What helps, though, is the realization of the second part of "letting go and letting God." The point is not just to let go, but to give control over to God. Most obsessive-compulsives will complain that if they do this everything will fall apart, but here is where faith comes in. God does not call us into ministry so that we can become self-sufficient in leadership. God calls us into leadership ministries to guide everyone together to serve God. As obsessive-compulsives we have to realize that our role is to lead others to serve God, and the only way to do that is through relinquishing all title to results. In other words, we have to simply let go.

Relinquishing requires a secondary task: spending more time in prayer as we give this ministry back to God. I think that obsessive-compulsives especially benefit from solitary and communal retreats where they are not in charge and have no duties. This time spent away from ministry has the power to help them realize that ministry goes on even without them, that God's work is not dependent upon them.

Self-Aware Leadership

We started the chapter by discussing how even the greatest leaders eventually are brought down by their spiritual and psychological pitfalls. It's unavoidable because no one is a complete package, and no leader has the skills to lead every kind of person. While our personality and style may appeal to some people, they will also turn off others. No one is a *complete* leader. Eventually our own incompleteness limits our leadership, just as our strengths build up our leadership. As people get used to us, they see our faults more and more, and these faults affect their response to us in ways that don't occur early on in our leadership.

With that being said, what then can we do to shore up our leadership? I believe that self-awareness—both psychological and spiritual—is essential. Too many church leaders live unexamined lives. They are only vaguely aware of their motivations, and so their darker motivations become driving forces in their ministries. The answer is to become involved in spiritual and psychological self-examination, and to engage in spiritual and psychological practices that balance us. Most spiritual and psychological disorders arise out of our self-consumption. In other words, whether from spiritual pride or a psychological personality disorder, over time we become more and more caught up in ourselves. Ironically, the more we get caught up in ourselves, the more we resist self-examination.

I truly believe that counseling and spiritual direction are the two most powerful tools to help people become self-aware. Both have benefited me. My training as a therapist required me to undergo years of supervision that had the effect of therapy, making me more aware of what my motivations were and are as a therapist. That self-awareness has been one of the greatest gifts, even if gaining it has been painful. I resisted my supervisors, yet their work with me allowed me to find ways to keep my own narcissistic, histrionic, borderline, and obsessive tendencies from tearing apart my ministry.

At the same time, I was supervised as a spiritual director and saw a spiritual director myself for years. Both helped me to become more grounded in the humble way of seeking God's will in everything, while simultaneously surrendering and relinquishing my ministry to God.

Ultimately, the point is that to become humble leaders, we have to be willing to explore and come to know ourselves. The more aware we are of ourselves, the more our ministry has the potential of being Christ's ministry, a humble ministry rooted in the Creator's purpose and supported by the power of the Holy Spirit.

3

Prayerful Leadership

❖

*He came out and went, as was his custom, to the Mount of Olives;
and the disciples followed him. When he reached the place, he said to
them, "Pray that you may not come into the time of trial." Then he
withdrew from them about a stone's throw, knelt down, and prayed,
"Father, if you are willing, remove this cup from me; yet, not my will
but yours be done."*

Luke 22:39–42

ARCHBISHOP OSCAR ROMERO STOOD AT A CROSSROADS. HE WAS
paralyzed with indecision. It seemed impossible to go back, but
what was the right path forward? Should he take the path of ca-
pitulation, choosing to work with a corrupt government that was
sponsoring terrorist attacks against its own people? Should he
stand up and speak out against the Salvadoran government, thus
assuring his own assassination? The people, and especially the
poor, were looking for him to do something, anything, to bring
an end to the violence.[1]

During the late 1970s and early 1980s, El Salvador was torn
by civil unrest. Right-wing death squads were torturing and killing hundreds and thousands of innocents. Left-wing communist
guerillas were persuading the poor to join them in their struggle
to overthrow the government. The government was so paranoid,
fearing that the poor would join the leftists, that they tortured and
killed many innocents as a way of intimidating the masses and
maintaining political power. Romero didn't know what to do.

Romero had been chosen archbishop of El Salvador precisely
because he was an orthodox, bookish, studious bishop whom the
other bishops believed would not make waves. Similarly, Romero

had no interest in fomenting trouble in the country. He wanted to lead the people of El Salvador back to an orthodox Roman Catholic faith. But when he was confronted with the reality of the violence against innocents, he knew he had to do something. He knew he was called to lead the people back to God's way, a way of love, compassion, forgiveness, and grace.

His dynamic transformation from a traditionalist, introverted, intellectual priest to a humble, activist archbishop came about after he toured El Salvador. He visited the sites where bodies of those executed by the death squads had been dumped. He visited men and women who had been beaten and tortured. He talked with officials from the government and with Marxist guerillas. He became fully aware that God was calling him to take a stand after an incident that revealed to him the evil afflicting El Salvador. He had negotiated the release of guerilla-held hostages after receiving promises from the Salvadoran army that they would not be mistreated. Despite these promises the guerillas (including a priest who had been supporting the guerillas) were immediately arrested. Romero also was arrested when he protested their treatment. In prison he heard the torture of the priest, and when he was released he was given the priest's dead body.

Romero was torn. He supported neither the Marxist guerilla rebellion nor the government-sponsored violence. He felt called to lead the people to a way of peace, but how could he do it? He knew that the way of violence pursued by both sides would lead to the spiritual and material destruction of the whole country. How could he lead the people to God's way—a way of love, justice, compassion, and unity?

Visiting the graves of victims of violence, Romero was stricken with grief. He stumbled forward along a road and then fell to his knees. He offered perhaps as profound a prayer as has ever been uttered: "I can't. . . . You must. . . . I'm yours. . . . Show me the way." He was brought to the depths of humiliation by his experiences, but in those depths he found the power of humility. Walking down the road into the poverty-stricken village nearby, he encountered soldiers. They mocked him, stripped him of his clothing. The poor rushed up to him and hugged his waist, embarrassed to see the partially naked archbishop being derided by the soldiers. Romero tried to quiet the people, telling them that everything was all right, but a woman protested, "But you are our voice. You speak for us."

Romero hesitated for a moment, not knowing how to respond, and then in humility he responded in the way that Christ called him to respond: "Let us begin a celebration of the Mass now. In the name of the Father, and of the Son, and of the Holy Spirit. Amen. The grace of our Lord, Jesus Christ, and the love of God, and the fellowship of the Holy Spirit be with you all. Lord, you have created us for freedom [and the people responded, 'Lord, have mercy']. Christ, you made us to live in dignity ['Christ, have mercy']. Lord, you strengthen us in the struggle for justice ['Lord, have mercy']." Romero rooted his response in sacramental prayer.

From that moment on, Romero spoke out against the government and the guerillas. He offered the country a new way, the way of Christ, the way of peace. He refused to be silent, even though his life was threatened. He gave a public homily on March 23, 1980, that was broadcast across the country. In his homily, he challenged the military to quit killing the poor and to bring justice to the country. He had sealed his fate. The military government could not let him continue speaking. The next day, as he celebrated Mass and held aloft the eucharistic chalice, two assassins crept into the church and shot him. They hoped to silence him, but in the end, they didn't. Moments before he was shot, he said these words, words that spread through El Salvador:

> Those who surrender to the service of the poor through love of Christ will live like the grains of wheat that dies. It only apparently dies. If it were not to die, it would remain a solitary grain. The harvest comes because of the grain that dies. We know that every effort to improve society, above all when society is so full of injustice and sin, is an effort that God blesses; that God wants; that God demands of us. I am bound, as a pastor, by divine command to give my life for those whom I love, and that is all Salvadoreans, even those who are going to kill me.[2]

His call for justice was taken up by the Salvadoran people, who eventually transformed the government and the country.

Romero was a wonderful model for those of us who aspire to be humble leaders, but not because of his particular political or religious beliefs or the principled stance he took. He was a model because his leadership was grounded in prayer. We cannot become humble leaders unless we are grounded in a prayerful pursuit of God's will. Romero was this kind of leader precisely because he prayed, and the more intense and confusing events became, the more intense his praying became. And this prayer opened him to a new way of seeing his role, a way grounded in the presence of Christ and the power of the Holy Spirit.

Humble leadership is always rooted in prayer because prayer puts us in a place where we can listen for and hear God. Jesus is the epitome of the humble, prayerful leader. To see evidence of his humility, you need look no further than the beginning of his ministry. When Jesus was baptized by the Holy Spirit, he had an experience that would have propelled any of us into immediate action. If I had been in Jesus's place, I would have emerged from the waters of the Jordan ready to change the world, ready to take on armies and emperors, ready to meet every challenge flanked by a host of angels. No one could have stopped me. But Jesus didn't operate that way. He was prayerfully humble. He followed the Holy Spirit into the desert rather than follow pride into the world. In the desert, he was forced to wrestle with the hubris that afflicts the rest and best of us. After he emerged from the waters, he followed the Holy Spirit into the desert instead of aggressively attacking the world's woes with his sword of justice. Why? So that he could pray and become grounded in the will of the Creator, not the will of human pride. And Jesus continued this humble prayer throughout his ministry. As a rule, whenever he did something great, he retreated into prayer.

The Gospels describe Jesus retreating for prayer time and again. Before choosing his 12 disciples, he spends the night in prayer (Luke 6:12). The transfiguration takes place while Peter, John, and James are with him on a retreat for prayer (Luke 9:28). After feeding the 5,000, Jesus goes off by himself to pray (Matt. 14:23). And as he faces his own arrest, imprisonment, torture, crucifixion, and death, he spends the night in the Garden of Gethsemane praying (Matt. 26:6–46).

What is it about prayer that makes it so crucial? Why can't we just lead from our own God-given reason, wisdom, insight, and ability? The answer comes from Paul. Paul was a great leader, but above all he was a prayerful leader. In his second letter to the Corinthians, he showed that the roots of humble leadership are in weakness and prayer. Paul describes how his faith and connection with Christ allowed him to see visions that no other person was permitted to see. He was elated and perhaps overconfident in his own abilities after receiving this vision. And so he was struck down with what he calls a thorn given to him in the flesh, "a messenger of Satan to torment me, to keep me from being too elated" (2 Cor. 12:7). Paul tells how he went to God three times in prayer, begging God to take his pain away, and in the midst of his prayer he heard an amazing response: "My grace is sufficient for you, for power is made perfect in weakness" (12:9). From that message, Paul discerned a path. He said, "Therefore I am content with weaknesses, insults, hardships, persecutions, and calamities for the sake of Christ; for whenever I am weak, then I am strong" (12:10). The way of prayer is the way of weakness.

Prayer weakens us, but not necessarily by taking away our physical, mental, or even political strength. It weakens us by centering us in God so that God's will becomes more prominent than our own. Prayer enables our will and God's will to come into alignment as we diminish our will, letting God's will become more influential. Of course I'm referring here to authentic prayer in which we truly seek God's will. Many pray but are inauthentic in that their prayer more resembles wishing or demanding than submitting. The more authentically prayerful we are in life, the more our hearts and minds naturally seek God's will and wisdom. I don't mean to say that just because we pray regularly, we automatically know what God wants in every situation. Ego and pride are still powerful forces, causing even prayerful people to mistake their own will for God's. The difference is that *humble* people of prayer increasingly become more willing to allow God's will to flow through them, rather than willfully assuming that their own will is God's will because of their own holiness. Humble prayer allows them to become more aware of how strong the power of pride is in life. It also causes them continually to question their own holiness.

A tremendous number of Christians, including Christian leaders, pray daily, read Scripture daily, and take their faith seriously but still remain willful. They are like the Pharisees who stand on the street corner, showing off how righteous they are by praying publicly and making a big deal about how hungry they are because they are fasting. But really their prayer is for show. Inside their focus is on themselves, not on God. In the same way, many Christian leaders pray, read Scripture, and do the right religious things, but at the core they aren't all that interested in what God wants. They project their will onto God, assuming that whatever they sense strongly to be right must be what God wants. They pray, but not from a humble posture, and as a result they never ask a basic question: whose will is this, mine or God's?

When we pray from a humble stance, an attitude of weakness that strongly desires to seek God's will but is also tentative about assuming with absolute certainty that we have discerned God's will, we are better prepared to discover God's pathways. If we come to prayer from a position of strength, assuming that God's will and ours are in alignment because of the strength of our faith, our practice of prayer, and our personal holiness, then we end up deluding ourselves.

Prayer is the primary pathway to humility, but only if it becomes an act of humility.

ROOTED IN EVERYTHING BUT PRAYER

Too much of contemporary Christian leadership is rooted in a soil other than prayer, even if it masquerades as prayer. You can see evidence of this phenomenon everywhere. In recent years I have witnessed many Christians leading from a quality other than prayerful humility, and the tragedy is that many Christians follow uncritically. Among the best examples I've seen of this attitude were comments from Pat Robertson, founder of the Christian Broadcasting Network and the Christian Coalition, in response to a string of criticisms against the United States by the Venezuelan president, Hugo Chávez. Believing that Chávez was a threat to U. S. interests, Robertson said during the August 22, 2005, broadcast of his television program, *The 700 Club:*

> Here was a popular coup that overthrew him [Chávez]. And what did the United States State Department do about it? Virtually nothing. And as a result, within about 48 hours that coup was broken; Chávez was back in power, but we had a chance to move in. He has destroyed the Venezuelan economy, and he's going to make that a launching pad for communist infiltration and Muslim extremism all over the continent.
>
> You know, I don't know about this doctrine of assassination, but if he thinks we're trying to assassinate him, I think that we really ought to go ahead and do it. It's a whole lot cheaper than starting a war. And I don't think any oil shipments will stop. But this man is a terrific danger and the United . . . this is in our sphere of influence, so we can't let this happen. We have the Monroe Doctrine, we have other doctrines that we have announced. And without question, this is a dangerous enemy to our south, controlling a huge pool of oil, that could hurt us very badly. We have the ability to take him out, and I think the time has come that we exercise that ability. We don't need another $200 billion war to get rid of one, you know, strong-arm dictator. It's a whole lot easier to have some of the covert operatives do the job and then get it over with.[3]

These are not the comments of a humbly prayerful leader. They are the comments of a leader who has made the tragic assumption that the United States' interests are automatically God's interests and that promoting assassination is a Christian act. There is no prayerful or biblical backing for this kind of position. I am not one to denigrate Robertson's entire ministry, but it becomes apparent at times that Christian leaders like him become intoxicated by their own influence and power and edge away from the humility Christ calls all of us toward. And he is not alone. Whether we are talking about conservative evangelicals like Robertson, or liberal progressives, it is very easy for

Christian leaders to lose their humility as their power and influence increases.

Ironically, even though the biblical example is of a leadership rooted in prayer, much of modern Christian leadership is grounded in some other soil. A powerful model for Christian leadership can be found in Acts. For example, right after the church is formed on Pentecost, we are told, "They devoted themselves to the apostles' teaching and fellowship, to the breaking of bread and the prayers" (Acts 2:42). Worship and prayer became the foundation of the leadership in the early church, and the ensuing stories of Acts tell us of miracles and wonders grounded in constant prayer and worship.

Unfortunately, too much of modern Christian leadership is grounded in three kinds of leadership that can mislead us, even if on the surface they appear to be Christian. These three are functional, traditional, and biblical leadership. All three forms can contribute to humble, effective leadership, but they cannot be the source of Christian spiritual leadership, because they are not always grounded in seeking God's will. This comment may sound odd, since biblical leadership is included in the list, but you will understand my meaning as we explore the three styles of leadership.

FUNCTIONAL LEADERSHIP

One of the best models of leadership is the corporate model. It makes sense that churches would look to corporations to teach us how to be effective leaders. This powerful style of leadership, which has emerged in North America and Western Europe over the past 100 years, especially in the U.S., has led to the highest level of innovation, organization, and production in human history. Business and corporate leadership is generally functional leadership. It is rooted in the pursuit of achievement, entrepreneurship, organization, exponential growth, and profit. The style emerged out of the Age of Enlightenment, attempting to incorporate an empirical and scientific approach that allows businesses to become ever more efficient and productive. It tries to develop economic, management, and production practices that will maximize production and profits while minimizing time and cost. Nothing wrong with that. This approach to leadership has allowed for the mass production of cars, televisions, housing, food, energy, entertainment, health care, and much more—developments that have increased our life expectancy, health, wealth, and leisure.

The problem is that functional leadership does not share the goals of Christian spiritual leadership. As Christian leaders, our goal is to lead people to seek and do God's will. That means doing God's will as individuals, congregations, and denominations. Fully applying the principles of functional leadership to the life of a congregation means substituting concerns for efficiency, production, time, and cost for seeking and doing God's will. God isn't as interested in forming efficient, productive, and cost-effective churches as in forming faithful, prayerful churches. God is after more spiritual aims: churches that promote the transformation and sanctification of human life so that all of us become new creations in Christ. What makes corporate leadership functional is that its focus is efficient performance, not the work of serving Christ.

Still, we can see the influence of functional leadership on the church. Often churches operate as though the pastor is CEO, the staff members are vice presidents in charge of this and that, and the members are both the factory workers and the product. What matters is getting the members to produce a commodity—and ministry, mission, and education constitute that commodity. Interestingly, the members can also be the commodity in churches whose main focus is numerical growth. The members become workers whose main role is to attract new workers so that the church can become larger, produce more programs, and increase its size and budget. Again, while corporate-style leadership can serve to make Christian spiritual leadership more effective, and while Christians should be encouraged to learn from the corporate world how to become better organized and more effective, functional leadership cannot serve as a primary leadership model because its goals are not the same as Christianity's goals.

Functional leadership skills and strategies can serve the humble leader but not vice versa. The humble leader has to serve God, not function.

TRADITIONAL LEADERSHIP

Certainly the traditions of the Christian church move us in God's direction. I believe that we ignore Christian tradition at our own peril. It is easy for succeeding generations to throw away the traditions of their forebears, assuming that only new ideas and approaches are best. Still, traditions last because they have been time-tested. They connect us with the wealth of ancient wisdom embedded in a faith. Tradition is different from custom. Customs are the specific practices passed down through the generations, practices that often emanate from tradition. Tradition is larger. It is the whole body of understanding and practice passed along from generation to generation.

For example, celebrating Thanksgiving is a tradition that is embodied in the custom of gathering with family and sharing a turkey dinner. Thus the customs are the meal and the emphasis on family, but the tradition is the emphasis on giving thanks to God as a sharing community, the reasons for the customs. We practice customs through the ages because we know that there is something deep and holy about them, and what is deep and holy are the traditions embedded in them, traditions that connect us with God's wisdom. Unfortunately, we often confuse the wisdom of the tradition with the practice of the custom, which causes us either to hold onto the custom as the only avenue to the wisdom of the tradition, or throw out the tradition along with the custom, thus robbing us of a tremendous source of ancient spiritual wisdom.

Over time, as cultures change and customs lose their relevance, it becomes difficult to discern what is the life-giving tradition and what is an *accretion*. Adrian van Kaam, one of the great writers on spirituality of the 20th century, helped me become aware of how accretions affect tradition.[4] An accretion is a distortion of a tradition that creeps in over time, or a distortion that develops because the original purpose or understanding of a tradition has been lost or forgotten or is no longer applicable.

It's a hard concept to explain, but not necessarily to understand. You've seen accretions in the physical world. If you accidentally leave a pot of water on a hot stove, boiling away all the water, the residue of minerals remaining in the pot is an accretion. When drinking the water, we don't see the accretions, even though we often purify water to remove them. The point is that unless we boil the water, we generally can't tell what is water and what is accretion. In a similar way, to determine what is simply accretion and what is life-giving tradition in religious leadership, we have to be willing to boil the tradition by asking searing questions about why we do what we do.

While religious traditions, and especially traditional leadership styles, can be life-giving, over time traditions develop residual customs, or accretions, that churches and denominations confuse with the spring of living water that feeds these traditions. Confusing the accretion with the living water, we begin to cherish the accretion more than the tradition. For instance, styles of music can become accretional. I notice this every time I choose hymns for Sunday worship. *The Presbyterian Hymnal* that we use contains more than 600 hymns, but only about one-third of them are appropriate for multigenerational worship. Why? Because many of the hymns were written before the 20th century and are difficult to sing for modern Christians who rarely listen to or sing classical-style songs. Older church members who grew up with them, and especially those who are classically trained, might cherish these hymns, but the hymns are considered difficult and archaic by many younger Christians who grew up listening to pop music. Still, there are rock-solid Christians who insist that any hymn written after 1876 is not *truly* sacred music and that sacred music written after 1880 is an abomination. The question is whether these folk are cherishing a deep Christian tradition of singing in worship, or cherishing an accretion that only classical-style music is appropriate for worship. The tradition of singing sacred hymns and songs is an ancient one that recognizes the power that music and congregational singing have to open us and connect us with God. The particular style of music is an accretion bound to certain periods of history.

We run into similar problems with accretions when leading other Christians. It is easy to confuse the accretional practices of Christian spiritual leadership with the life-giving tradition of leadership. Accretional leadership causes people to maintain tradition for tradition's sake. Such leadership is institution-driven. The focus is on maintaining the institution and its customs, rather than on using the deeper tradition to lead people to an encounter and experience of Christ. Accretional leaders operate in established ways, according to established protocols, without questioning whether these protocols still give life to a congregation.

A few examples make my point clearer. For instance, as a Presbyterian I have been given a wonderful tradition that guides me on how to lead. I am part of a denomination that is very democratic and believes strongly in following leadership processes that, it is hoped, will lead to a high rate of commitment and involvement by the congregation. Thus, as the pastor of the church, I cannot rule by fiat. Instead, I lead the church as its moderator and pastoral leader. I am responsible for creating a context in which the lay leaders, the elders of the church, make the decisions. My vote is only one vote among all votes on our church session (the Presbyterian term for church board). This is a wonderful tradition. Still, an accretion crept into this kind of leadership back in the 1970s. The focus then was on empowering the lay leaders of the church. The pastor's role increasingly was seen as that of a group therapist, guiding people to seek the answers that were already embedded within them.

This particular accretion, while emerging out of the democratic tradition of Presbyterianism as it came in contact with nondirective therapy, became an affliction that caused many pastors to feel guilty for actually leading. I know that it had a strong, negative impact on me early in my ministry. Each time I felt compelled to speak up and give guidance and direction in a session meeting, I felt guilty. Wasn't I supposed to let the elders come up with all the ideas? Wasn't my role simply to be quiet and help them figure out what to do? Even if they looked to me for answers, wasn't I supposed to empower them to be in charge and not just look to me? In the end, I discovered that this "nondirective" approach is a poor style of leadership. Even leaders look to leaders. Why would we diminish the insights and vision of those leaders, those pastors, who have been trained to offer spiritual insight and vision? To this day, this accretional style of

leadership persists in many of our churches. As a spiritual director, I've worked with quite a few pastors who have striven so
hard to empower other leaders that they refuse to give any guidance or direction. The result is either that the board leaders try
to fill the leadership void and end up in conflict over who is and
isn't in power, or the board becomes paralyzed, refusing to make
any decisions because they lack confidence in a direction. Please
don't misunderstand what I am saying. I'm not advocating that
we should be domineering leaders who do not empower. I just
believe that there is a balance between leading and empowering.

Another accretion in leadership that I've discovered over a
number of years while working with pastors and churches as
a spiritual director and guide has to do with the many restric-
tions our denominations have placed on who can and who cannot serve as pastor. The Presbyterian Church (U.S.A.), like many
other mainline denominations, has strict eligibility guidelines
on what qualifies a person to serve as the pastor of a church.
Many of these guidelines are good: graduation with a master of
divinity from an approved seminary, psychological well-being,
spiritual maturity, and more. Still, accretions have been built up
for reasons that may not always be the soundest. For instance,
in the Presbyterian Church (U.S.A.), an associate pastor who has
served with a senior pastor cannot succeed that pastor. The rule
was developed to protect congregations from feeling obliged to
hire a less-than-qualified associate to succeed the senior pastor.
While it prevents the church from being damaged by associates
who are not qualified to assume the mantle of senior pastor, it
also prevents qualified associates from maintaining continuity in
a congregation they already know and that trusts them.

Barring associates from succeeding pastors was born of the
bad experiences of churches that mistakenly hired unqualified
associates to be their senior pastor. Why prohibit someone who
knows the culture of a church, who has been part of its success,
and who has already formed relationships with the members,
from continuing the work already begun under the previous
pastor?

Many nondenominational churches have thrived by pursu-
ing the opposite strategy. Generally they groom associates to succeed senior pastors, much in the way that successful corporations

first look within for successors before looking outside. The associate already understands the successful church's culture and processes.

I have an acquaintance, a pastor who served a large church as an associate pastor for several years, the last six months of which he served with a new senior pastor. He then became senior pastor of a large church in the South, helping that church grow and become a dynamic place. When the senior pastor position at his former church became available, he considered returning, yet he was not eligible because of the few months he and the senior pastor overlapped. The rule against hiring previous associates was an accretion to the tradition that might prevent problems, but that also created obstacles for potential blessings. The tradition is that only qualified pastors should lead churches. The accretion is that serving as an associate with a senior pastor makes one automatically unqualified in that particular church.

Looking at the examples, you can see how traditional leadership can inhibit humble leadership when accretions build up and become confused with the traditions. Traditional leadership can be effective because it builds on what has been done well, but it cannot be a grounding, because it inhibits prayerful leadership by potentially making accretions more important than seeking and doing God's will. Traditional leadership can become a millstone that crushes creativity in a leader by turning the practices of the past into false gods that we must appease. Becoming a prayerful leader means asking God to help us to distinguish which parts of our traditions are helpful and healthy and which are merely accretions. In the end, leadership traditions can serve the prayerful and humble leader but not vice versa. The humble leader has to serve God, not a tradition.

BIBLICAL LEADERSHIP

It may seem odd to you, and even a bit blasphemous, to hear me say that biblical leadership can interfere with our ability to become humble, prayerful leaders. The sad truth, though, is that while following biblical principles of leadership can be extremely healthy and humbling, it can also be abused so that it creates an arrogant, prideful leadership style.

Biblical leadership is grounded in principles gleaned from a careful study of Scripture. Its power is that it attempts to ground leaders in seeking what God wants by almost scientifically elucidating a biblical standard of ethical and moral leadership. It also attempts to standardize a system of leadership that can be easily replicated by other Christian leaders. The problem is that while the Bible can offer principles of leadership, it doesn't necessarily connect us directly with God's voice and will. It is a step removed from humble, prayerful leadership. In fact, it can substitute the intellectual study of Scripture for a deep search for God's will in mind, body, heart, and soul. And if leadership is to be humble, it *must* be grounded in a desire to discern God's direct voice in moment-by-moment leadership.

Unfortunately, biblical leadership also can be abused by those who use the Bible to justify their own agendas. In many ways, the Bible is like a blueprint for a building. It gives direction and guidance—but situations and problems will arise that aren't covered by Scripture. We often end up having to make the wisest choices we can using Scripture as our grounding but also seeking God's direct guidance. Just as problems arise in construction that a blueprint cannot anticipate, leadership situations arise on which the Bible is silent. Many Christians apply the Bible in ways that it wasn't meant to be applied. They force it to fit where it doesn't fit. When that happens, forcing ourselves to follow biblical models inappropriately stifles creativity, especially prayerful creativity that arises in response to God's guidance. For example, as good a guide as the Bible is, it does not tell us precisely what the limits of a pastor's powers are, what kind of music a church should use in worship, and how to deal with a mentally ill person who is sowing division within a church. The problem of following the Bible is very similar to what happens when engineers and contractors use an architect's blueprints. Engineers and contractors sometimes must use their own training, intellect, and intuition to come up with creative solutions to problems architects did not anticipate. What would happen to a building if they ignored their own insights, training, and experience and stuck with plans that didn't take newer problems into account? In fact, what if they were forced to do so and were not even allowed to talk with the original architect to see what modifications could be made? This is often what happens with biblically based leaders. They pore over the Bible, using it like a blueprint, but then fail to engage in a creative dialogue with the architect—with God.

Good Christian spiritual leadership must be built upon a biblical structure, but it also must have a deeper foundation in humble prayer. Using the Bible as a blueprint without first being grounded in humble prayer creates conditions in which it can be misused to manipulate others. In contrast, the guidance of the Holy Spirit, which accompanies those who are humbly and prayerfully open, allows the Bible to become a wonderful resource for leadership. Prayer opens the Bible by connecting us with God's direct voice, which guides us as we lead a congregation through the difficulties all congregations face—difficulties not necessarily addressed specifically in Scripture. Obviously those pretending to be prayerful can also manipulate, but true prayerfulness leads people away from manipulation. In the end, biblical leadership practices can serve humble leadership but not vice versa. The humble leader must prayerfully serve God, not the Bible, which can become a God substitute. The Bible can lead us to God, but we cannot mistake it for God.

The functional, traditional, and biblical perspectives on leadership can be good resources for the humble leader, but ultimately all leadership must be grounded first in prayer if it is to become humble. The big question, then, is how we go about forming a prayerful foundation. What kinds of prayer practices do we engage in? Are there certain ways of praying that are more effective for leaders than others?

GROUNDED IN PRAYER

Do you know what the one big problem is with everything I've said so far? It's that grounding leadership in prayer is a great idea in theory, but the reality often gets in the way. How are we supposed to ground our leadership in prayer when we barely have time to think? How do we ground our leadership in prayer when we live in such a hectic world, a world that constantly stretches us in all directions? How are we supposed to be prayerful leaders when we don't really believe that we know how to pray—at least how to pray in a way that seems to work? How do we emphasize prayer in ministries in which those who are uncomfortable with prayer don't allow us to pray?

Increasingly, modern ministry is becoming bereft of deep, life-giving, and life-renewing prayer precisely because we live in a functional culture, driven by technology, schedules, and computers; a culture that moves at a faster and faster pace, driving out time for prayer and reflection. Pastors may pray, but that prayer is often ceremonial and given in a public context, not devotional prayer offered in a private or communal context. Ironically, the effect on churches, the very institutions that are supposed to lead us away from being formed by the culture, and into a life of prayer, is that they become completely functional places driven by technology, schedules, and computers. Spiritual leaders feel as though they do not have time to pray. I struggle with this time bind constantly. I am the pastor of a growing church, and growing churches are always organizations in which the challenges of programming, organizing, administering, visiting, counseling, teaching, preaching, and leading create the conditions in which prayer and reflection are pushed to the margins. The problem is that all of these facets of the vocation scream for attention, demanding our immediate attention, while prayer barely whispers to us that it is time to pray. It's easy to ignore the call to prayer in the face of such demands.

Perhaps the real problem isn't all these demands but rather our resistance to prayer. For whatever reason, prayer is hard for most of us. I've studied the spiritual writings of great thinkers on prayer for most of my adult life, and one thing I consistently notice is that they all believe prayer should be as natural as breathing. All agree that prayer is essential to Christian life. And all agree that prayer is extremely hard because we resist it. It may be as natural as breathing, but if that's the case, most of us must suffer from spiritual asthma. We resist making the time to pray.

We resist making the space for prayer. We resist the feelings of discomfort that always arise when we pray—feelings that our prayer is inadequate because we don't know the right ways to pray; that our prayer is foolish, infantile, and unable to rise to the level of eloquence that God certainly must require in order to pay attention to us; and that our prayer ultimately focuses either on things that God is too busy to pay attention to or things that we are selfish for asking. So we don't pray. We give in to the seductive voice that says, "You're far too busy for the luxury of prayer."

So how do we ground our leadership in prayer when we face so many external and internal pressures against prayer? We do it by seeking ways to make prayer as natural as breathing. I certainly believe that time spent in formal, disciplined, structured prayer is important, especially if we are beginners in prayer. I believe that if we are new to prayer, we need to practice prayer disciplines such as intercessory prayer, confessional prayer, centering prayer, and contemplative prayer. That said, I am going to assume for this discussion that you are familiar with these practices and have some experience with them. If you are not and believe that you need help in these areas, I encourage you to follow this endnote for some suggested resources that have helped me in my own prayer life.[5]

Most spiritual leaders, especially pastors, even those who are trained in the spiritual disciplines of prayer, find it harder and harder in modern life to stick with a discipline of prayer. The truth is that our parishioners won't tell us to take more time for prayer. They may tell us that we need to devote more time to visitation, sermon preparation, administration, or communication, but not prayer. So how do we ground our humble leadership in prayer as it becomes increasingly difficult to devote time to prayer? I believe the answer is to make prayer more natural and less disciplined. In many ways the practice of prayer is similar to the training an athlete goes through. For example, the professional football player doesn't spend countless hours running on the road, doing wind sprints, and lifting weights just for the sake of being stronger and fitter. The football player does these things because they help him play football. They are disciplines that support his natural abilities. I believe that this same principle applies to the prayer disciplines. Spiritual disciplines are not ends in themselves. They are disciplines that support the life of prayer. When they become ends in themselves, then they become problems because we can end up serving the disciplines rather than God.

What do I mean by this statement? I had a discussion years ago with a classmate in graduate school while I was studying spirituality and prayer. She felt a calling to a life of prayer. She is what we call a "contemplative." In our discussion, she kept telling me that all of us are called to be contemplatives, and if we are not spending at least 30 minutes to an hour a day in contemplative prayer, then our ministries are serving ourselves, not God. I'm not sure where she came up with that formula, but it made perfect sense to her because she couldn't do her work without spending 30 minutes to an hour in prayer each day. The problem was that I wasn't sure I had the same calling, and her formula made me feel guilty. I was practicing contemplative prayer 30 minutes a day, but it was a struggle. I tend to be a restless person. My body wasn't designed for that kind of inactivity. I grew up as an athlete, always moving, always fidgeting.

I suppose the contemplative response to this objection might be that I just need to become more centered so that I become less fidgety. The problem is that I know in my heart of hearts that this answer is false. I was created a certain way with a certain psychophysiological temperament. To force me to make contemplative prayer my main practice is to force me to become a square peg in a round hole. Does that mean I shouldn't practice contemplative prayer? No. I do practice it and have for years. Some years I am more disciplined, some I am less. (As the father of young children, I also know from experience that small children are not always interested in our prayer practices, especially when they want a snack, have to go potty, or are squabbling with a sibling over a toy.)

Thus, my point to my classmate was that not all of us are called to the same prayer practices. Unfortunately, one tendency of Christians is to state that certain theological perspectives, worship styles, prayer practices, or musical preferences should be adhered to by everyone. We have many prayer practices to choose from, however. Whatever disciplines we practice, they are meant to get us into spiritual shape so that we can form a relationship with God that allows us to lead with humility and openness to God's voice and direction.

That being said, I believe that there are two ways of grounding leadership in prayer. Both are more "natural" ways of praying— ways that seem to give life to Paul's advice to the Thessalonians that they should "pray without ceasing" (1 Thess. 5:17). The first of these was discovered and taught by a relatively obscure 18th-century monk named Brother Lawrence. Brother Lawrence was the epitome of humility. He was not a great leader, although he led people to spiritual depth. He was not a great practitioner of any particular prayer discipline. In fact, he had a reputation for falling asleep during the community's regular prayer times, which consisted of reading and reflection upon the Psalms. He found that his attempts at contemplative prayer left him frustrated because he always got distracted. The other brothers quickly discovered that Brother Lawrence was also not particularly endowed with what we might today call "spiritual gifts." In other words, he didn't do anything particularly well. So his task was to keep the kitchen clean. It was while sweeping the floors and cleaning the pots that Brother Lawrence developed a simple prayer practice that gave life to Paul's guidance to "pray without ceasing." Brother Lawrence developed a style of prayer that he called *practicing the presence of God*.

The practice is fairly simple. As Brother Lawrence wrote to one of his friends:

> We do not have to be constantly in church to be with God. We can make our heart a prayer room into which we can retire from time to time to converse with Him gently, humbly and lovingly. Everyone is capable of these familiar conversations with God—some more, some less. He knows what our capabilities are. Let us begin, for perhaps He is only awaiting a generous resolve on our part.[6]

Practicing the presence of God boils down to keeping a running conversation with God going throughout the day. We ask

God to guide or help us when we are confused, uncertain, or out of ideas. We thank God when we discover that God has providentially helped the work of a project. We thank God when we discover that God has given us an insight or the ability to articulate a difficult thought when counseling others. We thank God when we discover that God has providentially caused something to happen that helped us solve a problem, reconcile a relationship, or perform some other seemingly coincidental act that changed the dynamic of a situation or our ministry. We listen for God's whisper to reveal to us what God wants us to say in our sermon, how God wants us to resolve a conflict, or what direction God wants us to lead the church.

Practicing the presence of God is simple, although it does require one major commitment from us. We have to actually believe and treat God as though God is with us. We have to believe that God permeates everything and everyone. To practice the presence of God means to treat God as though God and we are not separate but are united in a divine union. We may not be God, and God may not be us, but certainly Christ is incarnated within us, and the Holy Spirit surrounds us and acts through us.

Second, to bring the practice of prayer even deeper into our leadership, the Quaker writer Thomas Kelly has revealed an even deeper way to unite our hearts and minds with God, and that is to prayerfully *let the presence of Christ flow through us.* Kelly says:

> Deep within us all there is an amazing inner sanctuary of the soul, a holy place, a Divine Center, a speaking Voice, to which we may continuously return. Eternity is at our hearts, pressing upon our time-torn lives, warming us with intimations of an astounding destiny, calling us home unto Itself. Yielding to these persuasions, gladly committing ourselves in body and soul, utterly and completely, to the Light Within, is the beginning of true life. It is a dynamic center, a creative Life that presses to birth within us. It is a Light Within which illumines the face of God and casts new shadows and new glories upon the face of men. It is a seed stirring to life if we do not choke it. It is the Shekinah of the soul, the Presence in the midst. Here is the Slumbering Christ, stirring to be awakened, to become the soul we clothe in earthly form and action. And He is within us all.[7]

According to Kelly, Christ is already a presence within, a presence we can awaken and that can live and act through us. Most of us, even the humblest, tend to look at our ministries and leadership as our own. We generally see what we do as serving Christ, much as a servant serves a master. Certainly being a servant to Christ in ministry is biblical, yet this model of ministry can disconnect us from Christ by making our ministry, and especially our leadership, something we do *for* Christ. A deeper biblical perspective is Kelly's insight that sees Christ *within* us ready to lead *through* us. It is a model based on John 15:1–11, where Jesus tell us:

> I am the vine, and my Father is the vinegrower. He removes every branch in me that bears no fruit. Every branch that bears fruit he prunes to make it bear more fruit. You have already been cleansed by the word that I have spoken to you. Live in me as I live in you. Just as the branch cannot bear fruit by itself unless it lives in the vine, neither can you unless you live in me. I am the vine, you are the branches. Those who live in me and I in them bear much fruit, because apart from me you can do nothing. Whoever does not live in me is thrown into the fire, and burned. If you live in me, and my words live in you, ask for whatever you wish, and it will be done for you. My Father is glorified by this, that you bear much fruit and become my disciples. As the Father has loved me, so I have loved you; live in my love. If you keep my commandments, you will live in my love, just as I have kept my Father's commandments and live in his love. I have said these things to you so that my joy may be complete in you, and that your joy may be complete.

This perspective recognizes that Christ is alive within us, filling us with grace, and working through us by using our minds, mouths, hands, and feet. When we have this perspective, we recognize that prayerful leadership is a matter of opening up within to Christ, who is already there. Opening up to Christ is deeper than simply carrying on a conversation with God all day long. It is being in, with, and for Christ in everything we do. We engage in what psychiatrist and spiritual teacher Gerald May calls *willingness*.[8]

When we are "willing," we let Christ's will flow through us. We engage in a life of prayer that allows our will to resonate with God's will. We continually open our minds, hearts, and souls to God, so that God's will can more fully act in and through us. As we do this, our whole lives become prayer. As David Steindl-Rast, a writer in prayer and spirituality, says, "True people of prayer need to say fewer prayers than others, because their life *itself* is prayer, is practice. There is a misconception that the more time you spend saying prayers or doing meditations, the better. My contention is, the less you need, the better."[9] As humble leaders, we aim toward the union of our minds with God's mind. Ultimately, we want to lead from God's will rather than our own, but to do so requires a humility that leads us to continual prayerfulness, and a continual prayerfulness that leads to humility. There is no way to describe a three-step or any-step process that leads to this kind of leadership. It simply emerges out of a willingness to reach inside, to awaken the slumbering Christ who is within, to live in that "amazing inner sanctuary of the soul," that "holy place" and "Divine Center" where we can continually discover the "speaking Voice" Kelly described above. This is the Divine Center out of which humble leadership emerges, a Center discovered as we allow our leadership to be transformed by prayer into prayer.

STEEPED IN GOD'S GUIDANCE

Prayerful leadership reaches deep into the Center by steeping us in a process in which we constantly seek God's voice. The point of prayer is not only to unite our hearts, minds, and souls with Christ but to follow the will of Christ by continually seeking, searching for Christ's voice. Leadership that is prayerfully discerning breaks the rules of our culture. North American culture is a problem-solving culture that analyzes problems and develops solutions to the problems. Humble Christian leadership appraises problems and then discerns answers to the problems. There's a world of difference between the two.

The process of analysis entails figuring out an answer by tearing apart a problem or situation, looking at the relationship of the parts, and then figuring out a new way to fix or reconstruct it. This style of problem-solving lies close to the root of the word "analyze," which comes from the prefix *ana* ("up") and the Latin root *lysis* ("to loose or split"). In other words, when we analyze a problem, we loosen up or split something up to study the components. We study how they interact. We study them as individual components. Once we spot the problem in the component or the relationship, we then come up with a solution to "fix" it. There's nothing inherently wrong with analyzing a problem to come up with a solution. It's what we Americans do best, and it's what makes our technology, creativity, and innovation the envy of the world. The problem is that it is a wholly human endeavor. It relies on rational analysis and logical deduction. It doesn't leave room for prayerfully seeking God's answer. Imagine entering a business meeting and saying, "Certainly your analysis of the problem is good, but we need also to consider God's perspective." After the perplexed looks, what would happen next? I don't advocate getting rid of analysis completely. Analysis can serve discernment by helping people understand an issue. What I am advocating is relegating rational analysis to its proper place, which is to support the deeper practice of discernment.

As humble, spiritual leaders we are called to do more than analyze problems and lead congregations toward solutions. We are called to lead people into discernment, and the movement into discernment begins with us as leaders. We have to be humbly discerning leaders. To understand what that means, it helps to look at the French roots of the word "discernment." It comes from the prefix *dis* ("apart") and the root *cernere* ("to separate"). In essence, discerning is "separating apart" a situation to determine what is junk and what is good. It is like sifting for gold. Discernment is prayerfully sifting through alternatives and possibilities to uncover the gold hidden within. The gold is God's answer, an answer that may correspond with a careful analysis but that also may seem illogical and irrational.

To be a discerning leader means to lead in a way that encourages people to eschew quick analysis in favor of prayerfully sifting for God's answers. I encourage you to explore some of the many excellent resources on discernment. Among the best are these:

- *Discerning God's Will Together* by Danny Morris and Charles Olsen.
- *Discerning Your Congregation's Future* by Roy Oswald and Robert Friedrich, Jr.
- *Discerning God's Will* by Ben Campbell Johnson.
- *Scripture and Discernment: Decision Making in the Church* by Luke Timothy Johnson.[10]

Making discernment central in our lives and leadership helps us to become more fluid, enabling us to discover solutions to problems and avenues of possibility that more functional, traditional, and even biblical leaders otherwise miss. Too many leaders in today's mainline churches, facing obstacles such as shifts in demographics and religious preferences, don't know how to react. They become paralyzed by these obstacles and in the process become like lava rather than water. What do I mean by this? Do you know the basic difference between water and lava? Though both are liquid, their freezing points differ. It doesn't take much of a drop in temperature for lava to stop flowing and become solid. Think about hot lava rushing from the mouth of a volcano downhill after an eruption. If it hits a big and seemingly insurmountable obstacle, it will at first try to push against it or burn it away. Its nature is to flow. Gravity compels it to flow. But if it cannot get by, through, over, or around an obstacle, it will eventually cool. As it cools, it becomes solid rock, thus making the obstacle even bigger. Lava, facing a seemingly insurmountable obstacle, becomes an obstacle itself.

Too many of today's mainline religious and pastoral leaders are like lava. We encounter an obstacle in religious or church life, and if we can't get around it or remove it by our own strength, we eventually get stuck. We get stuck behind the obstacle by accepting it as permanent and unassailable. The modern mainline church is filled with examples of churches and their leaders solidifying behind obstacles. The fact that our denominations are so much like lava explains why we are often stuck and continue to decline. The overwhelming majority of our congregations are likewise stuck and in decline.

Look at all the issues our denominations are perpetually stuck on: homosexuality and homosexual ordination; conservative, evangelical orthodoxy versus liberal, progressive theology; pro-life versus pro-choice stances; the Great Commission versus the Great Command; and tradition versus innovation. Our local congregations also demonstrate a similar paralysis: contemporary versus traditional music; mission to the unchurched versus mission to the poor, oppressed, and marginalized; appeasing the older members versus reaching out to younger generations; growth versus stability and intimacy; and tradition versus experimentation.

Our leadership at denominational and congregational levels has becomes like lava, and so our denominations get perpetually stuck on seemingly irresolvable issues. We become paralyzed. We stake out our positions, basing them on functional, traditional, or biblical positions, and then get locked into never-ending arguments that drain our energy, resources, and creativity. The more we get stuck in never-ending fights over the same old topics, the less ability we have to respond to the needs of the world. We end up creating more obstacles by never allowing resources and energy to transform our churches so that they actually reach people where they are. We fight constantly over topics such as homosexuality and orthodoxy, pouring all of our resources into the fights and draining energy and vision from other crucial ministries. We believe that we can't get over, around, or through these obstacles, and so by becoming frozen in our positions, we end up increasing the mass of the obstacle. We don't see alternatives, so we become convinced that the only answer is our answer, the only solution is our solution, the only path is our path, and that those who disagree with us are our enemies.

We often become like lava when we can't see a way around an obstacle, whether it is practical, relational, or theological, and then obsess about the obstacle until we increase the size of the obstacle. We end up contributing to obstacles through our attitudes and practices. Some of us become resigned, bitter, cynical, or angry and therefore become leaders who drain the energy of our church members. Or we may become apathetic leaders who feel consigned to our fate, allowing our congregations to atrophy. Or in most cases, we simply become hapless, helpless leaders who long ago stopped being creative. We fill a pulpit but don't lead from it. We moderate meetings but don't lead them. We teach people but don't guide them to new ways of responding to life's problems. We don't like where we are, but we don't see any options. So we stay where we are, and through our increasingly negative attitudes, we slowly become an obstacle to others. We stand in the way of others who may be creative and energetic.

Lava leadership has petrified mainline churches and denominations. Who has the energy to overcome denominations and churches led by lava-like leaders? I believe that the refusal to imitate the frozen leadership of the mainline denominations has led to much of the growth of the nondenominational movement. Most nondenominational megachurches are led by leaders who became frustrated with denominational lava leaders and decided to seek their own way rather than become lava leaders themselves.

Water reacts differently from lava to obstacles. Water may get stuck behind a barrier for a while, but eventually it does one of three things: it finds a way around it; it rises, transcends, and overcomes it; or it erodes it. Water always searches for a way, and it never stops. Water constantly searches, reaches, explores, and finds new avenues and paths. Even if it gets frozen for a season, it will eventually thaw and again begin seeking an alternative way. When we are like water as leaders, we creatively seek ways around obstacles, refusing to get stuck.

Discerning leadership is *water leadership*. Hannah Hurnard, in her book *Hind's Feet on High Places*, offers a poem about water cascading down a mountain and becoming humble, a poem that reflects water leadership, describing water as the epitome of humility:

> Oh, what joy it is to race
> Down to find the lowest place.
> This is the dearest law we know—
> "It is happy to go low."

Sweetest urge and sweetest will,
"Let us go down lower still."[11]

To be a discerning leader is to be like water as we ever more
humbly seek God's guidance and direction. No matter what obstacles we face as leaders, there is a way around, over, or through
the obstacle, and God wants to reveal it. But to discover it, we
have to be willing prayerfully to discern God's avenues. Often
that means being willing to consider any possibility and to subject it to God's guidance. Water seeks other possibilities. A pool
of water will send out tentacles, exploring every possibility. If
it finds a channel, it will flow into it. If that channel, too, turns
into an obstacle, the water will still explore it fully before flowing in another direction, toward another possible conduit back to
the main pool. Eventually the water will find a tiny channel and
begin, slowly at first, to trickle through it. Over time, the flow of
water will make that channel larger and more easily traversed.

I see this kind of water flow all the time in our congregation.
The leaders of our church—lay, staff, or pastoral—almost never
reject a possibility out of hand. For instance, as our youth group
grew beyond the ability of our youth director, Bruce Smith, to be
everywhere and do everything, he recognized a wonderful potential. Expanding the youth program to include fifth and sixth
graders, he asked the eldest members of the senior-high youth
group to become the youth-group leaders of the fifth- and sixth-
grade group. We offered internships to college students, training
them to be youth leaders. We hired a seminary student to train,
supervise, and encourage the older youth to become leaders for
the younger kids. In the process, we gave the younger kids wonderful teenage models. We taught leadership skills to the older
teens—skills that we hope in the future they can translate into
water leadership to lava-led churches and denominations. Thus,
we train future leaders for the church.

Discerning leadership is water leadership. It constantly and
prayerfully seeks God's will and way. It also encourages others
to do so too. Water leaders teach other leaders to become like water rather than like lava. Water pastors help lava-laity to become

fluid and hopeful, seeking creative solutions to the problems that plague them and their churches.

PRAYER IS EVERYTHING IN LEADERSHIP

For the humble leader, prayer is everything. It is the air we breathe that allows us to discern God's purpose, become open to God's presence, and become alive to God's power. Prayer connects us to God the Creator, allowing us to discern and follow God's calling for our congregations, callings that are tied to God's deeper purpose for our churches and us. When we immerse our leadership in prayer, we constantly seek and listen to God's call—a call that opens us to the path God has set for us.

Prayerful leadership connects us with the presence of Christ who is always in our midst, leading and guiding us to freshness and newness. Humble leadership recognizes that we are not alone in our ministries, serving a distant master. We are servants serving Christ who is in our midst—Christ who lets us be his body both as individuals and as a community. Prayer connects us with this indwelling and incarnate Christ who wants to be the vine that sends grace flowing through we who are branches. When we are prayerful leaders, we lead out of a vibrant connection with Christ that leads our congregations to recognize and live out of that connection,

Finally, prayerful leadership makes us alive to the power of the Holy Spirit that is always vibrantly present in our communities. Even if a church has been frozen in place through years of lava leadership, the power is still there, ready to be discovered as water leaders surface who show us how to wear down the layers of rock, allowing this providential power to emerge. This power of providence is always there when we are humbly open to it. Most often this power is manifested in coincidences.

Adrian van Kaam said something in a class I took with him many years ago, and it has affected my leadership and life profoundly ever since. He said, "There are no coincidences, only providences." In effect, he was saying that we may look at situations and write them off as mere coincidence, but the prayerful, humble leader recognizes them as pure providence. The Holy Spirit is always seeking ways to bring this power into our midst. I've noticed that with astounding regularity the Holy Spirit acts in my life in providential ways. When a need arises in our congregation, the Holy Spirit leads me to a member who has skill or experience in addressing it. When the church grows to a certain point, members join who have experience guiding churches through organizational growth. When I'm stuck myself, God uses members of the congregation who gently remind me that God is present. When I pray, I discover providence already in my midst. My role as a leader often is just to be prayerfully aware of what God is already doing, of the opportunities God is presenting us, and to lead people to consider, explore, and embrace those possibilities.

Prayerful leadership is leadership that opens us to God, who wants our churches to do well.

4

Unifying Leadership

—•— ⫙♦⫙ —•—

I therefore, the prisoner in the Lord, beg you to lead a life worthy of the calling to which you have been called, with all humility and gentleness, with patience, bearing with one another in love, making every effort to maintain the unity of the Spirit in the bond of peace. There is one body and one Spirit, just as you were called to the one hope of your calling, one Lord, one faith, one baptism, one God and Father of all, who is above all and through all and in all.

Ephesians 4:1–6

THE WORDS ABOVE ARE A POWERFUL REMINDER OF OUR CHRISTIAN calling. Paul packed a lot into such a short paragraph, telling the leaders of the congregation in Ephesus what their goal should be and how to get there. The Ephesian church had mostly Gentile converts, who were unfamiliar and a bit uncomfortable with the Jewish customs surrounding the congregation's worship and organizing structure. These people could easily have fallen prey to the division and infighting common in so many of the early churches. In fact, Paul was well aware that several of the churches he had started or visited were torn by conflict. The church in Corinth was one. It had all sorts of divisions, enough that it required Paul to write several letters to them telling them how to become united in one body. A spirit of division had become so ingrained in them that they were developing formulas for who was or wasn't a true Christian. The formula was simple for some. They considered themselves to be true Christians because they followed the teachings of a dynamic preacher named Apollos. Others claimed that they were truly Christian because they were followers of Paul. The church in Galatia was another church divided by different forces, some of whom attacked Paul personally, saying that Paul was not a true apostle.

Even in the original church, forces were at work dividing Christian against Christian. Reading Paul's letters gives us the impression that many in the early church were divided against each other and that the early church was hardly harmonious. The apostles had to work very hard to lead the church to spiritual and practical unity.

We live in divisive times today. Everywhere you look there is division, with no apparent end in sight to this divisive spirit. I believe that one reason George W. Bush won the electoral college in 2000 was his promise to the people that he was a uniter, not a divider: "I showed the people of Texas that I'm a uniter, not a divider. I refuse to play the politics of putting people into groups and pitting one group against another."[1] Five years later, a CNN/ *USA Today*/Gallup poll was taken on the eve of President Bush's 2005 inauguration for a second term. The question was whether President Bush was a uniter or a divider. Amazingly, and ironically, the poll showed tremendous division in the country over the question of division. Forty-nine percent responded that President Bush was a uniter. Forty-nine percent said he was a divider.[2]

How can a country be so evenly split over such a simple question? Doesn't this poll result automatically implicate the leader, indicating that he is a divider? Not necessarily. The truth is that we live in divisive times. Over the past decade or more, our population has been completely divided in many ways. U.S. leadership has reflected the divisions of our culture politically, generationally, racially, religiously, and denominationally. We have been a politically divided culture of red and blue states, whose leaders have believed that the answers to life's problems lie in either conservative or liberal solutions. Looking at our population from a generational perspective, we are divided into five age cohorts—the G.I., silent, baby boom, gen-X, and millennial generations—each of which approaches life in very different ways. We are a racially divided culture of African Americans, Hispanic Americans, European Americans, Native Americans, Asian Americans, Middle Eastern Americans, and more, each bringing different ethnic perspectives to life. We are a religiously divided culture of Christians, Jews, Muslims, Buddhists, Hindus, agnostics, atheists, and others, all claiming that their own religious perspective is *the* perspective. And even within Christianity we are a denominationally divided culture of Eastern Orthodox, Roman Catholics, and Protestants; progressives and evangelicals; mainliners and Pentecostals, each clinging to a strong religious tradition with sometimes conflicting priorities. We live in a culture that is finding it hard not only to live with each other but also to live with the rest of the world. There is division between the United States and the Middle East, the United States and Europe, and indeed, the United States and much of the world.

Our political, racial, religious, and diplomatic divisions have had a cost. A large percentage of our population does not trust the government, or any large institutions, for that matter. We live amid deficits and debt that no one wants to address. A tone of acrimony permeates our political life.

This same division is alive and well in many of our churches. Too many of our churches are divided by issues large and small, whether homosexuality, abortion, worship music, or the color of the carpeting in the sanctuary. This division has led to distrust, decline, and bitterness in our denominations.

It's almost as though there is something in the water we are all drinking, causing us to divide over everything. How did we get here? How did the spirit of divisiveness infect our culture and our churches, spreading like a virus and causing Americans and Christians to see only what is wrong in each other and not what's right? Considering Paul's words at the beginning of this chapter, how did we get to this point that we don't seek to live in humility and gentleness? Why don't we seem to care about having patience and bearing with one another in love? Why can't we make every effort to maintain the unity of the Spirit in the bond of peace? I see a pervasive divisiveness, one echoed in the words of the evangelical Pat Robertson: "You say you're supposed to be nice to the Episcopalians and the Presbyterians and the Methodists and this, that, and the other thing. Nonsense. I don't have to be nice to the spirit of the Antichrist. I can love the people who hold false opinions, but I don't have to be nice to them."[3] How closely do these words adhere to the ideals set forth by Paul in our opening Scripture?

Perhaps the biggest factor in this divisiveness is that our leadership generally lacks the humility needed to unify. We live in a time in which we have an overabundance of arrogant leaders. This arrogance is bipartisan and multidenominational. Leaders in every walk of life today are convinced that their way is the only way and that those who block the way are also blocking God's will and way. A tangible pride among too many political and religious leaders causes them arrogantly to assume that they are the only true carriers of truth. Often the name they give their version of truth is the "pursuit of purity." As one pastor told me, "Love and all that is OK, but what we really need is a return to purity. That's what Jesus wanted: purity."

The prideful leadership of many of today's leaders is the polar opposite of the kind of leadership Paul envisioned, not only for the church in Ephesus but for all Christians. He spoke of leadership in a church that leads to "humility and gentleness, with patience, bearing with one another in love, making every effort to maintain the unity of the Spirit in the bond of peace." Too many in our culture, and especially in the church, have lost sight of Christ's brand of leadership, which is grounded in servanthood and humility. As he taught his disciples after washing their feet, "So if I, your Lord and Teacher, have washed your feet, you also ought to wash one another's feet. For I have set you an example, that you also should do as I have done to you" (John 13:14–15). This is the example of leadership set by Christ. It is a humble leadership, a servant leadership, and a unifying leadership. It calls on leaders to put their own interests and pursuits in the service of Christ's.

We live in divisive times, but as leaders we are called to rise above this division and truly to become uniters, not dividers, for *humble leadership is unifying leadership.* Unifying leaders lead people to seek a common good that is rooted in God's good. They are called to put aside their own desires for power, control, and dominance and to seek what is good for everyone. But they are not called simply to compromise or to lead people to a kind of bland sameness in which everyone is bound to a common good that really is no good. The drive to such a false good was the essential problem with Marxism. In practice, Marxists protected people from the destructive side of capitalism, but by doing so, they also insulated the people from prosperity, plunging the whole populace into a kind of mediocrity and collective poverty. Its purpose was to bind people together on the basis of a humanistic common good. Unifying, humble leadership seeks to bind people to a common good, but it is God's good. Its aim is to lead people to live in holy community and to find a way gently and lovingly to guide people in that direction. Finally, unifying leadership seeks to lead people to a common experience, a spiritual experience of Christ in community as together we seek God's way for us.

THE ROOTS OF OUR DIVISION

Some sources of division are always present to a degree. Others appear like cyclical plagues of locusts. Looking at all of them together, we can see that overcoming division is a daunting task.

GENERATIONAL DIVISION

I wish I could put the blame for our culture's division squarely on our national politics, but the blame doesn't belong there. Neither the Republican nor the Democratic party is the source of our division. Rather the parties embody deeper existing divisions. In many ways, our cultural division reflects a much deeper generational discord. I believe we are divided now precisely because baby boomers have assumed the leadership mantle, and members of this generation have always sown division, even when trying to promote unity. For instance, when boomers were young adults, they often promoted their own unity with the motto "Never trust anyone over 30."

Why am I so critical of boomers? Technically, I am a boomer, so in criticizing them, I'm implicating myself. But the truth is that I'm not down on boomers so much as I am simply aware that the boomer generation has spent most of its existence divided against one thing or another.

The boomers, born in the years from 1943 and 1960, began as one of the most indulged generations in American history.[4] It was a generation that came of age after the Allied victory in World War II during a time of great optimism. In contrast to their parents, who were part of the G.I. and silent generations (born in 1901–1924 and 1925–1942, respectively), generations that emphasized community and civic unity, the boomers grew up as an individualistic generation. They grew up being somewhat narcissistic, expecting the culture to revolve around them. They have always been a spiritually hungry generation, seeking spiritual answers in music and drugs, Eastern religions and philosophies, and eventually in evangelical and Pentecostal Christianity. As they have moved into their 40s, 50s, and 60s, members of this generation have become increasingly moralistic and moralizing, chastising younger generations for the very behaviors that they forgave in themselves at the same age. As business, political, and religious leaders, they have been a compelling and energetic generation that has often erased limitations and boundaries, creating limitless access to all information through the Internet, becoming the most mobile generation within the United States, spreading Christian faith far and wide, and feeling free to dabble in the affairs of other countries, whether by invitation or not. They have often been visionary, offering new visions for overcoming age-old problems. They are a generation that grew up disillusioned with the culture in general and institutions in particular. During their formative years they witnessed the assassinations of John and Robert Kennedy and Martin Luther King, Jr., as well as the corruptions of Watergate. The pain and disillusionment of these experiences led them to become skeptical of institutions. They also rejected their parents' music, culture, and religion, and then set about to create their own, developing musical styles from rock to rap that still dominate popular culture.

On the downside, the boomer generation has been one of the most divisive generations in history, certainly the most divisive in the United States since the mid-1800s, when a similar generation, which William Strauss and Neil Howe call the "Transcendental" generation, grew into young adulthood and fanned the flames that sparked the Civil War. That was a generation of idealists (Henry David Thoreau and Ralph Waldo Emerson) as young adults and political zealots in middle age. As Strauss and Howe's studies reveal, an idealistic, boomer-like generation emerges about every 80 years in American history, creating the context for divisiveness that often leads to conflict and even an unraveling of the society, in both the secular and religious worlds. For instance, the rise of a spiritual renewal seems to take place about every 80 years as an idealistic generation comes into young adulthood, seeking spiritual meaning. Generally, it begins as a spiritual seeking that later leads to a Christian renewal.

The first American generational cohort that initiated a spiritual renewal was the Puritan Awakening, which took place between 1621 and 1640. The next renewal was the Great Awakening (1734–1743), the first major American evangelical movement, which occurred in New England, sparked by clergyman Jonathan Edwards. The Transcendental Awakening took place between 1822 and 1837 as Americans were introduced to a new spiritual vision through the writings of Emerson, Longfellow, and Thoreau; this era later gave way to the Second Great Awakening in the mid-19th century. The Missionary Awakening took place between 1866 and 1903, as America became consumed with reshaping the world, as evidenced in the writings and teachings of people like William Jennings Bryan, Billy Sunday, Frank Lloyd Wright, Albert Einstein, and Douglas MacArthur. This missionary zeal also led to another Christian Awakening with the rise of the Pentecostal movement in the early 20th century. The baby-boom awakening (1967–1980) came as a generation of youth sought deeper meaning by dabbling in drugs, countercultural music, and psychological and spiritual exploration. Later, the seeking of the '60s and '70s sparked the rise of Christian evangelicalism in the 1980s, 1990s, and the first decade of the 21st century. The spiritual seeking and renewal of Idealists is usually accompanied by their pitting themselves against the dominant culture, causing division, until they themselves become the dominant culture and then aggressively turn against anyone who would threaten their dominance. You can see this division in the political culture sparked by the rise of such boomer politicians as Bill Clinton, James Carville, Lee Atwater, Karl Rove, and George W. Bush.

According to Strauss and Howe's research, it seems almost inevitable that when an idealistic generation hits middle age and its members become leaders, they also lead the culture into division. And right now boomers not only dominate the political leadership of our country; they have also become the central generation of leaders in our churches and denominations. In fact, since very few generation X-ers have chosen to be involved in the present-day church and prove to be difficult to entice into our congregations, we often are left with boomer leadership. Boomer leaders can be both a blessing and a curse. Boomers are the most creative leaders, often finding new solutions to intractable problems. Yet their drive to be creative, new, and relevant often pits them against other generations—meaning that their leadership can be shackled with an us-versus-them mentality that sparks conflict.

The point is that we seem to be caught in the grips of a generational configuration that almost guarantees division. Strauss and Howe tell us that when American culture has an idealistic generation like the boomers in leadership, the country typically goes into a period of unraveling. We experienced great unravelings before in the American Revolution, the Civil War, and the twin crises of the Great Depression and World War II. Often the Idealists lead us into a time of crisis, although this development is not inevitable. On the other hand, while they may lead us into crisis because of their divisiveness, Idealists also have a sense of spiritual wisdom that eventually leads people to a sense of unity.

Just as Franklin Delano Roosevelt, a member of an idealistic "Missionary" generation, united the people of this country at the onset of the World War II, we can hope that boomer leaders will eventually have the spiritual wisdom to lead us into great unity, both in our country and in our churches. This wisdom won't come, though, until boomer leaders recognize that they are called to be humble, unifying leaders.

IDEOLOGICAL DIVISION

It's not just generational factors that have given rise to divisive leadership. We are also plagued by ideological conflict. We are a culture divided by ideology in a way that is reminiscent of Jesus's times, when the Jews were divided. There was division between Sadducees, who believed in a strict observance of the Law with no room for interpretation, and Pharisees, who followed the Law but allowed new ideas to be integrated into their faith. Division existed between Zealots, who fought against the Roman occupation of Jewish lands, and the temple priestly class, who accepted Roman rule and made accommodation with it. Division was prevalent between Jewish separatists and accommodationists—between Jews who believed in strict separation between Jews and Gentiles and those who actively courted trade and interaction. Division was common between those who held to a strict Jewish faith and those who integrated the insights of Greek philosophy. And even among the early Christians, divisions existed between those who believed that the Law required the circumcision of all converts and those who didn't. Everywhere one looked, ideological divisions could be found.

We also live in a time of ideological division. In our denominations, a strong line of division separates Christians over matters of practice, belief, and perspective. Some divisions are deeper than those separating Republicans and Democrats, progressives and evangelicals, Protestants and Roman Catholics. They are central to the truths we hold to be self-evident.

The biggest Jewish division during Jesus's time was the Sadducee/Pharisee conflict. The Sadducees were a movement within Judaism that believed in strict observance of the law with no allowance for interpretation—we might think of them as the fundamentalists of their day. They didn't believe in life after death, they didn't believe in living with or mixing with Gentiles, and they didn't believe in synagogues—only in worship revolving around the Temple. The Pharisees were the liberals of their day. They observed the law strictly, but with some interpretation. For example, they believed that the faithful would be physically resurrected after death, that Jews could live among and trade with Gentiles, and that synagogues could augment temple worship. In fact, the present-day Jewish faith is grounded in the Pharisee tradition, which survived after the Temple was destroyed in 70 CE.

While the Sadducees and Pharisees were divided over interpretation, they held the same basic ideology. They both embraced a principle that today we call "works righteousness." Works righteousness is the attempt to work out our salvation by trying to perfect and purify our actions. In other words, by trying to adhere perfectly to God's law, we hope to overcome the breach between God and humanity and to make ourselves pure enough to merit God's forgiveness and salvation. Both the Pharisees and the Sadducees offered a works-oriented path to salvation. Jesus overcame this division by offering an alternative: he spoke against all forms of works righteousness and instead taught an alternative path that depended upon God's love and grace for salvation, not on the purity of our works.

Despite Jesus's emphasis on love and grace, we still struggle with works righteousness in the church today. In fact, historically we have always struggled with it. It was grappling with the Roman Catholic Church's embrace of works righteousness that caused Martin Luther to spark the Protestant Reformation, as he emphasized God's grace over the works-righteousness practice of indulgences. This practice arose out of the 16th-century Roman Catholic teaching that certain monetary contributions to the church had the power to save us. The ideological struggle between works righteousness and reliance on grace caused massive divisions in Europe during the 16th and 17th centuries, and even though the Protestant revolution maintained that it rejected works righteousness in favor of faith and grace, the denominations ironically continued to fight over what practices—the Eucharist, certain forms of baptism, Scripture reading, church attendance—had the power to save us, or at least to connect us with Christ's saving grace. We still grapple with works righteousness any time that the religious suggest that by being members of a particular church or denomination, by engaging in certain spiritual practices, or by being involved in certain ministries or missions, we are assured of our salvation.

Still, among contemporary Protestants an even more subtle ideological seduction creates division. I would call it "beliefs righteousness." Most Protestants have too much awareness of the pitfalls of works righteousness to allow it to become a pervasive

source of division, but they are not aware that beliefs righteousness has created division in the contemporary church. Beliefs
righteousness is the subtle and seductive idea that the purity of
our beliefs can save us. It is based on the idea that if we know
the Bible well enough, know sufficient Christian doctrine and
theology, and have a strong and pure orthodox belief, we can
merit our own salvation. You can see how the subtle seductions
of beliefs righteousness infect our church like a virus, causing
evangelicals to suspect progressives of not being Christians or
"saved," and tempting progressive Christians to believe that the
rigid beliefs of evangelicals are evidence that they are not "truly"
Christian. We are in the midst of a massive fight between parties
of beliefs-righteousness Christians as they try to determine who
is and who isn't Christian, who is and who isn't an enemy, who
is and isn't "saved."

I saw a perfect example of beliefs righteousness in a colleague
of mine upon his becoming a pastor in my presbytery—which is
what we Presbyterians call our judicatory associations of churches. This pastor was examined by our presbytery's pastors and
elders, and in the process he said of himself, "The thing I like best
in ministry is to teach unbelievers and new Christians what they
need to know to be saved." This is a statement reflecting beliefs
righteousness. Nowhere does Scripture tell us that there is something we need to "know" to be saved. In fact, Paul, in his letter to
the Romans, goes to great lengths to tell us that grace is the only
thing that can save us. Our faith links us to that saving grace. He
does not tell us that the purity of our beliefs saves us. As Paul
says, "For there is no distinction, since all have sinned and fall
short of the glory of God; they are now justified by his grace as
a gift, through the redemption that is in Christ Jesus . . ." (Rom.
3:22–24). Paul goes on to say, "Therefore, since we are justified
by faith, we have peace with God through our Lord Jesus Christ,
through whom we have obtained access to this grace in which
we stand; and we boast in our hope of sharing the glory of God"
(Rom. 5:1–2).

Paul implies that even if we believe the wrong things, if we
have faith in Christ, it links us to God's grace, which saves us.
Faith is trust, and our trust and surrender to Christ opens us up

to receive the gift of grace. Just as Jesus often told people after healing them, "Your faith has made you well," our faith makes us receptive to grace. As the Quaker mystic Hannah Whitall Smith said, "Your salvation comes, not because your faith saves you, but because it links you to the Saviour who saves; and your believing is really nothing but the link."[5] Beliefs righteousness, the tendency to link having the right theological beliefs with salvation, is a contemporary form of an ancient heresy called Gnosticism. Gnosticism was a first-century belief that this world is corrupt and that the only thing that can lift us to the stainlessness of the heavenly realms is learning certain secret beliefs that purify us and enable our souls to rise above our corrupt human bodies. John's Gospel is written mainly in opposition to a Gnostic brand of Christianity. He writes about *believing* in Christ, using Gnostic language, but he is really trying to implode the Gnostic separation of spirit and body by showing that belief in Christ allows Christ to be in us and us to be in Christ. John's concept of belief was what we call "faith."

I will also mention one other form of "righteousness" that afflicts the modern church, although its divisive power is not as apparent in the mainline church because it is part of a movement that, by and large, is not part of the mainline Christian mindset. This form of righteousness is "gifts righteousness," and it is apparent among charismatic and Pentecostal Christians. Christians beset by gifts righteousness emphasize such gifts of the Spirit as speaking in tongues, interpreting tongues, prophesying, healing, and engaging in holy laughter. They suggest that a Christian's failure to exhibit one of these or several other gifts is evidence that the person is not saved.

All of these forms of "righteousness" lead to ideological divisions based upon claims to having the right Christian theology and ideology. They take many forms, and proponents of each are convinced that their ideology leads to purity, but in the end it mainly leads to division as Christian divides against Christian, and Christian divides against non-Christian. These ideological divisions turn Christian faith into a battleground for supremacy over ideals. The result of these divisions is that Christians within denominations and congregations have a difficult time uniting—a state of affairs that makes being a unifying leader very difficult.

Great Command/Commision Divisiveness

A third form of division among Christians is the false dichotomy between choosing to follow the *Great Command* or the *Great Commission*. In many ways, this seems to be the dominant division between evangelicals and mainline moderate and progressive Christians. Most mainline moderates and liberals emphasize the Great Command in their ministries. The Great Command is, "You shall love the Lord your God with all your heart, and with all your soul, and with all your strength, and with all your mind; and your neighbor as yourself" (Luke 10:27). Following this command, many Christians see their primary calling as loving God and loving others.

In contrast, many evangelicals see the primary calling as following the Great Commission, which is Jesus's final teaching at the end of Matthew's gospel. Jesus says, "Go therefore and make disciples of all nations, baptizing them in the name of the Father and of the Son and of the Holy Spirit, and teaching them to obey everything that I have commanded you" (Matt. 28:19–20). For evangelical Christians, this is a clear call to reach out to and convert non-Christians. Great Command Christians often see Great Commission Christians as being aggressive, arrogant, and prideful. Great Commission Christians often see Great Command Christians as being false and impure in doctrine, failing to serve Christ faithfully, and weak in faith. This division causes Christians generally to look upon each other with suspicion, distrust, and sometimes outright scorn.

A History of Conflict

The divisions in our church today concern belief, tradition, ministry and mission emphasis, and much more. We also struggle with a historical problem. We Americans seem to have been born and bred in conflict. Those at odds with their home countries and nations came to America to escape religious and political persecution. They set up colonies around their own belief systems and often persecuted those who were not like them. For instance, Massachusetts was a land for Puritan and other Calvinist Christians. Rhode Island was a safe haven for Quakers. Maryland was a colony for Roman Catholics. The United States of America was founded in conflict through the revolution against England. We fought a terrible and bloody Civil War that tore at the fabric of our culture and was never quite healed. In fact, if you look at a map of the red-state/blue-state division in our culture, it is disturbingly close to Southern/Northern state division of the Civil War. How do we overcome conflict when it seems almost to be coded into our culture's DNA?

Humble leadership has a lot to overcome if it is to be unifying. It has to overcome generational, ideological, cultural, and historical factors. It is a hard task, but at the same time, truly humble leadership holds the key to unifying. It is grounded in Christ, who ultimately always overcomes division.

SEEDS OF UNITY

Unifying leadership is planted when we root our leadership in Scripture, especially in the model of Jesus, for he is the epitome of the unifying leader. Although he was hunted and hated by Pharisees, Sadducees, and Romans, he was able to unite a diverse set of followers. Among his followers were fishermen, shepherds, tax collectors, zealots, pacifists, the wealthy, and the poor. He brought together a group of people who otherwise would have had little to do with each other, and he united them in following God's ways.

What did Jesus do specifically to unify those around him? Jesus's leadership seemed to focus on three unifying principles— principles that I believe we can replicate in our own leadership. These three were *calling, grounding,* and *binding.* First, Jesus led out of a sense of *calling.* We are told that immediately after his baptism, Jesus heard the call of the Spirit, and followed it into the desert. Earlier, I said it was a sign of Jesus's humility to follow the Spirit into the desert, but it was also a testimony to the roots of his unifying leadership. The wilderness was a place to clarify his purpose and calling. The experience of the wilderness forced him to look deep into his mind and soul, but also to struggle with the demonic. In the biblical tradition the desert has always been the place of purifying and transformation. Others, like Moses, the Israelites, David, and Elijah, had been led out into the desert to be transformed as they discovered both God and their calling. In the same way, Jesus had to fight with the power of corruption that wants to tear apart the unity between us and God, us and others, us and ourselves. It is the power of the demonic that entices us to choose our own way instead of God's and thereby to bring division into the world. In the end, Jesus resisted temptation precisely because he was clear about his purpose and calling.

These two—purpose and calling—are not necessarily the same. Our purpose has to do with God's intent in creating us. Each of us has been created with a specific purpose in mind. Each of us has a basic reason for being, whether or not we choose to recognize, accept, and root ourselves in that reason. While we can never quite articulate that purpose, we know whether we are living according to it. When we are not living according to our purpose, life becomes hard. We feel confused and somewhat chaotic. We sense that something is missing, but we don't know what. And searching for it doesn't necessarily reveal it because our purpose isn't as much "out there" as it is "in here."

Our purpose is embedded in our DNA. It's for that reason that people seem to be genetically attracted to and adept at certain activities. For example, some people seem to be born to play football, soccer, hockey, baseball, or basketball. Others seem genetically predisposed to be photographers, artists, parents, cooks, writers, leaders, mechanics, actors, servants, sellers, buyers, doctors, lawyers, pilots, counselors, builders, or preachers. Not everyone feels this same sense of deep passion, but each of us does have a purpose. For these people, capturing a sense of purpose can be difficult, especially if other circumstances play a part, such as troubled childhoods, addictions, and a desire for things that abiding by our purpose may not bring, such as wealth, fame, and power. Whatever our purpose, it reflects not only our interests, but also our physical, mental, and emotional talents. Our purpose is like the theme of our lives. It tells us what our life story should be.

The problem is that just as the theme of a story is hard to capture in reading the story, ascertaining our purpose is hard to capture while living from day to day. What exactly is our purpose? The answer to that question always remains elusive. In contrast, our calling is much clearer, even if it may be somewhat hard to ascertain at times, especially if we aren't used to seeking God's call. Our calling literally is how God is telling us to articulate our purpose concretely and pragmatically in a particular phase or period of life. It is the voice of God "calling" us to do this, try that, follow this path, or walk in that direction. Our purpose is the theme of a story. Our calling is like the particulars of the plot. It is the unfolding of the theme in concrete events and experiences. The different phases of our lives are like the chapters of a story—chapters that reveal how we are called to live life in response to certain events, situations, and challenges. In some lives, the chapters contain twists and turns. In others, the chapters are much more placid. So, transposing this concept to our lives, our purpose is our life theme or plot, but our calling is how that theme is lived out in concrete situations.

To live life in consonance with God, we need to listen for and follow God's theme in each phase of our lives by seeking how God is calling us to act on that theme in a given situation. Jesus himself did that. Following the Gospel story, you can see how Jesus, acting from his purpose as savior, also seemed intuitively to understand what each phase of his ministry required. He led from his own calling to make others aware of their callings. Leading from our calling, out of how God is telling to lead others, is a key to unifying leadership. When we are unifying leaders, we help people listen to and hear their call, but we do this first by becoming clear about our own calling. In essence, when determining what our goal should be in any leadership situation, we need to be seeking God's will, not the congregation's will. Especially in pastoral leadership, the temptation is strong to lead the congregation in a direction it wants to go rather than the one God is calling the members to go, the direction in which God is calling us to lead them. For instance, many pastors take congregational surveys to get a sense of the direction in which they should lead the congregation. The problem is that this method doesn't necessarily reveal where God is leading the congregation. Following a survey can cause a congregation to remain stuck in the past. The pastor who seeks God's call for the congregation is better equipped to lead the congregation in the direction that God wants it to go. Leading out of a sense of what God is calling us to do is the difference between real leadership and reactive leadership. When we are truly leading people to move in God's direction, we follow where we discern God is calling us to lead them. When we lead reactively, we do what the congregation wants us to do without asking if this path is really God's will.

Even though we follow and are able to articulate to others what God is calling us to do, it doesn't necessarily mean that the church members will automatically follow. Often people resist God's call. For instance, sometimes Jesus articulated God's call and saw his leadership rejected. Matthew tells the story of a rich young man who comes to Jesus and asks him what he must do to have eternal life. The young man declares that he has been able to keep all the commandments. What else is there to do? Jesus says, "If you wish to be perfect, go, sell your possessions, and give the money to the poor, and you will have treasure in heaven; then come, follow me" (Matt. 19:21). The young man goes away grieving because he has so much and is unwilling to give it up.

You can hear in this story the struggle to follow God's call. The young man feels that his purpose was to live a God-centered, righteous life; in keeping with that purpose, he followed the call to keep the commandments. So Jesus further called him to follow the path to an even richer life, selling all that he had and becoming a follower of Jesus. The young man wouldn't follow that call, and he grieved because he knew that he was rejecting not only his call, but a piece of his purpose. He could still seek the righteous life, but he could go no further until he embraced Christ's call.

The point is that Jesus not only led from his own calling, but he taught others to listen for and follow their callings. Not all were prepared to follow, but that didn't prevent Jesus from calling others to seek and follow God's will for them.

As leaders, we are called to educate others to follow their calling. We do not provide that call—a truth that some leaders conveniently forget. Too many bad leaders, especially leaders of cults, try to substitute their own self-focused calling for God's call. I've run into that temptation in my own ministry. For instance, what do we do with members who are unhappy in our churches? Do we determine for them that their calling is to stay, even if they are unhappy? What I've always tried to do is to encourage those called to Calvin Church to be involved in Calvin Church, but I've also come across members who have said that they just don't feel that they fit at Calvin. In those cases I've sat down with them and tried to help them discern what kind of church they feel called to be a part of. I make suggestions, sometimes sending them to churches that I myself don't like much because of their theology or worship styles, but I do so knowing that my unhappy members will be happier there. In several cases I've privately commissioned them, praying with them and telling them that I consider them missionaries from Calvin Church who can help make another church a healthy congregation.

I believe that we can't be unifying leaders with people who feel at a fundamental level, even if unconsciously, that they are not called to be a part of our congregations. It becomes destructive to manipulate them into staying. Unfortunately, in a world where size seems to be all that matters, letting people go to follow their calling can seem counterintuitive. If we really believe that the church is the body of Christ, then we need to encourage people to become part of the congregations with which they fit, for no local church alone can be the sole body of Christ. The true body of Christ is made up of Catholic, Protestant, Pentecostal, evangelical, mainline, conservative, and progressive churches. We may not believe that, but that's because we tend to overvalue one part of the body while undervaluing another. I believe that Christ values all parts of the body, and the failure of our churches to become unified has more to do with the failure of our leaders than with one or another church being "right" and the others "wrong."

A second way that Jesus led was from a sense of *grounding*. He always remained grounded himself, and he kept his disciples and followers grounded. Being grounded means remaining rooted in what matters, such as God, relationships, and humility. Keeping his disciples grounded was no easy task, because they had plans. They had ambitions. They were always striving to use their discipleship to their advantage. For example, James and John got their mother (the wimps!) to ask Jesus if they could be his right- and left-hand men when Jesus brought God's kingdom into the world (Matt. 20:20–23). The other disciples were furious at them for having the temerity to suggest such a thing. Jesus, always seeking ways to keep the disciples grounded, used the moment to teach them what was important. He said to the disciples, "You know that the rulers of the Gentiles lord it over them, and their great ones are tyrants over them. It will not be so among you; but whoever wishes to be great among you must be your servant, and whoever wishes to be first among you must be your slave; just as the Son of Man came not to be served but to serve, and to give his life a ransom for many" (Matt. 20:25–28).

Good leaders keep their followers grounded, especially grounded in God, by constantly teaching them what is expected, what is accepted, and what is rejected. They make clear what is expected by constantly pointing out what is essential and what isn't. It's very easy for Christians to get caught up in all the peripheral "stuff" of Christianity and to forget what's important, especially what is important in church life: we are the body of Christ, and we are always to maintain unity in the Spirit. This is *grounding* for church life and leadership.

To ground the church, we have to help people remember that the church is the body of Christ. Paul uses this metaphor for the church in his first letter to the Corinthians. He writes, "For just as the body is one and has many members, and all the members of the body, though many, are one body, so it is with Christ. For in the one Spirit we were all baptized into one body—Jews or Greeks, slaves or free—and we were all made to drink of one Spirit. Indeed, the body does not consist of one member but of many" (1 Cor. 12:12–15). This is a profound statement, because it emphasizes that everyone, even one with whom we completely disagree, has a part in the life of the church. It also suggests that healthy leaders unify that body, finding a way to help all body parts work together. Good leaders find a way to bring these parts together, so that everyone's talent builds up the body of Christ. And they do it by helping their members consider their calling while grounding them in a sense of purpose.

To ground the members of the church, we leaders have to help the members remember that we are to seek unity in the Spirit. It isn't enough just to be unified; we need to form a sort of divine union with each other and with God through the power of the Holy Spirit. As Paul says, "I therefore, the prisoner in the Lord, beg you to lead a life worthy of the calling to which you have been called, with all humility and gentleness, with patience, bearing with one another in love, making every effort to main-tain the unity of the Spirit in the bond of peace. There is one body and one Spirit, just as you were called to the one hope of your calling" (Eph. 4:1–4). Paul's guidance brings the leader back to humility and prayer. We cannot unify people in the Spirit unless they are also prayerfully open to the Spirit. The leader's role is to ground people in the Spirit by making them aware that the Spirit is always among us, binding us, working in us, transforming the world through us. But to have this unity of the Spirit requires that we lead out of humility, gentleness, and patience, always bearing with other's faults, and in this way lead people to seek God's will.

The third unifying principle of Jesus's leadership is that it was *binding*. Jesus bound people to God and to each other. And in his final commissioning of the disciples, he called them to a binding ministry—to go and make disciples of all people (Matt. 28:19). Love is the binding power of the church. As John says, "Beloved, let us love one another, because love is from God; ev-eryone who loves is born of God and knows God. Whoever does not love does not know God, for God is love. . . . God is love, and those who abide in love abide in God, and God abides in them" (1 John 4:7–8, 16). I've noticed as a spiritual director and counselor with pastors and church leaders, and in reflection on my own ministry, that problems almost always begin when lead-ers forget to love. The more focused they become on themselves, their agendas, the success of their church or ministry, or their own importance, the more they forget that their primary purpose is to love, at least according to what John says in the passage above. It is easy for leaders to forget how important love is. The pressures of leadership often cause leaders to feel alone and unappreciated, and over time, they can burn out.

Recently, much attention has been paid both to the factors that lead to burnout in leaders, and to the role love has in restoring a sense of purpose and satisfaction among leaders. In their groundbreaking study *Resonant Leadership*, Richard Boyatzis and Annie McKee, researchers in organizational behavior and leadership, discuss how constant self-sacrifice can erode a leader's confidence and effectiveness, erosion that begins as the leader loses a sense of love and compassion. As they say:

> But when leaders sacrifice too much for too long—and reap too little—they can become trapped in what we call the *Sacrifice Syndrome*. Leadership is exciting, but it is also stressful. And it is lonely. Leadership is the exercise of power and influence—and power creates distance between people. Leaders are often cut off from support and relationships with people. Our bodies are just not equipped to deal with this kind of pressure day after day. Over time, we become exhausted—we burn out or burn up. The constant small crises, heavy responsibilities, and perpetual need to influence people can be a heavy burden, so much so that we find ourselves trapped in the Sacrifice Syndrome and slip into internal disquiet, unrest, and distress.
>
> In other words, *dissonance becomes the default,* even for leaders who *can* create resonance. And, because our emotions are contagious, dissonance spreads quickly to those around us and eventually permeates our organizations.[6]

The term *resonance,* as these authors use it, refers to the ability to inspire hope in the face of fear and despair, to bring people of varying backgrounds and talents together in a sense of consonance. In their research, they found that most truly exceptional leaders are *resonant leaders,* leaders who

> are in tune with those around them. This results in people working in sync with each other, in tune with each others' thoughts

(what to do) and emotions (why to do it). Leaders who can create resonance are people who either intuitively understand or have worked hard to develop emotional intelligence—namely, the competencies of self-awareness, self-management, social awareness, and relationship management.[7]

Resonant leaders know how to move out of the Sacrifice Syndrome, a malady that afflicts many congregational leaders, especially pastors. Those afflicted with Sacrifice Syndrome become bitter over time at the church's seeming unwillingness to follow their vision, especially in light of the many sacrifices they have made for their ministry. Many pastors quietly die inside as they constantly sacrifice their own will, finances, personal time, families, and even health for their congregations, hoping to turn their churches into dynamic centers of God's activity. They burn out because they sacrifice themselves not only for others but also for God. And when they receive few tangible rewards, they succumb to Sacrifice Syndrome.

What enables leaders to overcome Sacrifice Syndrome? Restoring *compassion*, say Boyatzis and McKee. They might be reluctant to use the term love, but compassion as they describe it is a significant portion of love. As they say, "When we experience *compassion*, we are in tune with people around us. We understand their wants and needs, and we are motivated to act on our feelings. Like hope, compassion invokes renewal in our mind, body, and heart. And, like hope, compassion is contagious."[8] By becoming more compassionate toward those we are leading, we enhance our resonance with others by emphasizing relationships, not production, as the foundation of work. As Boyatzis and McKee point out throughout their work, leaders who emphasize production, effectiveness, and efficiency often get none of these. Those who emphasize relationships create the conditions for greater production, effectiveness, and efficiency. For example, they reflect on the failures of one particular man they studied, a man who was sent to a third-world country to organize the economic efforts of a nongovernmental agency:

In essence, Eduardo totally missed the *emotional reality* of the community and the country. He was under a lot of pressure to

get results and did not see that *relationships* were the currency
and the vehicle for change in this setting. He did not see that
when people met to discuss strategies, they were doing at least
two things at once: finding common ground so that they could
make decisions, and healing the wounds of the past. What he
dismissed as meaningless "chicken parties" were actually a
key means for bridging the gaps of understanding between the
previously opposing sides. He totally missed the fact that relationships needed to be healed and rebuilt—*before* any formal
plan could be conceived. And as the pressures mounted and
the complexity of the situation increased, his intense focus on
outcomes as opposed to relationships became more and more
ineffective.[9]

In effect, they say that Eduardo lacked compassion for those
working under him. He was too focused on the project rather
than the people. The way Boyatzis and McKee define compassion, it is clearly part of Christian love, yet Christian love goes
further. As 1 John reminds us, God is love, and therefore when
we love others, we are not only acting with God, but we are also
incarnating God. Love means acting in consonance with God so
that God's grace fills us and flows through us to the other. God's
grace also returns to us through the other.

True love for another allows us to move into mutuality, a relationship in which we cherish others and they cherish us. Love
breaks down the tendency to treat others as either facilitators or
obstacles to our goals. I believe that this tendency to treat the
members and leaders of our churches as either facilitators or
obstacles to achieving our vision is a huge problem in today's
church. Too many pastors are driven by their ambitions and see
people as cogs in the machine of progress. If a pastor becomes
successful, he sees the members as good cogs who did their jobs
well, responding to his designs and plans. If a pastor believes
his plans and designs are resisted and thwarted, then he sees
the members and other leaders as bad cogs—as faulty parts that
should be either replaced or removed.

Love overcomes the tendency to see others as parts in a religious machine by enabling leaders to regard members and other
leaders as companions rather than cogs. The word "companion"

is a wonderful Christian word, because it literally means to "eat bread with" (com-"together with," and panis-"bread"). A companion is not only a person with whom we are willing to share a meal, but in the sacramental sense, a person with whom we share communion. When we lovingly consider the members and other leaders as companions, then we are willing to share ourselves with them. We break out of the need to dominate or control them. We share life with them, the life of Christ. Seeing others as companions allows us to break out of Sacrifice Syndrome by rooting us in God's way and will while also allowing God's love to flow through our leadership and ministry. The practical side of grounding our leadership in love is that as leaders we must work on always emphasizing love and on finding ways always to treat those around us with respect, compassion, and forbearance. Unfortunately, many leaders feel free to treat both staff and members coarsely out of disrespect, fear, and a need for control.

Despite everything I've said, binding our leadership in love does not prevent us from ever coming into conflict with others or keep us from becoming irritated with or even disliking others. Binding leadership in love simply means that we strive to care about everyone, even those with whom we are in conflict or whom we dislike.

In my own experience as a pastoral leader, I can tangibly see the effects of love as well as the impact of failing to love. I was heavily influenced by a talk I heard years ago by Frank Harrington, then pastor of Peachtree Presbyterian Church in Atlanta, Georgia, the largest church in the Presbyterian Church (U.S.A.). He told us that loving our congregations was the most significant thing we could do as pastors and related the story of a young pastor he had met who asked him to speak at his church in Oklahoma. Harrington accepted the invitation, expecting to speak to a large church somewhere outside Oklahoma City, since he mostly spoke at large church gatherings.

The young man picked Harrington up at the airport and drove him several hours out into the country, all along exclaiming how wonderful and great his church was, and how it was on the verge of a tremendous renewal. Harrington kept expecting to come across a large church, but as they continued to drive past suburbs and small towns, deeper and deeper into the country, he realized that he was heading to a church very different from the ones he normally spoke to. When they finally arrived, he discovered that the church was a simple, tiny, country church that had saved up for over a year to be able to afford Harrington's speaking fees. Harrington told us that the pastor's love for that church was tangible, and that it was a tremendous church, albeit small. Harrington discovered in that moment that it wasn't the size of the church that mattered, but the strength of its love. He told us that if we love our churches, whatever size they are, they can become dynamic places of grace and God's presence and power.

I've taken Harrington's words to heart, and I can see a tangible difference in my ministry. Whenever my love for my congregation is strong, I notice that the church feels more dynamic and filled with God's presence. When I become more self-consumed, complaining to myself about the lack of this or that in the church, I notice that the church seems to lose steam. Not to sound too egocentric, but I've noticed that my love for the congregation seems to bind the church to God. When my love is lacking, things in the church begin to feel "loose" and disconnected.

Ultimately, calling, grounding, and binding all work together. The more we lead from our own calling, calling others to follow their call, the more our leadership grounds the church in God's work and will. And the more grounded in God the congregation and I am, the more we both seem to find love easier.

PRAGMATIC UNITY

So far we've dealt with leadership in a somewhat abstract manner, talking about principles and foundations upon which humble, unifying leadership needs to be built. Principles and foundations are important, but even the most principled leader can fail if she doesn't have the practical skills to unify people. It is the pragmatic that attracts me so much to the Gospels and to Jesus's teachings. Jesus was principled, but he was also pragmatic. Jesus did simple, concrete things to unify his disciples and his followers.

Over the years I have been taught practical skills for creating cohesion in families, groups, and organizations. I wish that I could say that I learned these skills in seminary, but the truth is that my seminary training was mostly abstract and theological. In fact, while I was in seminary, one of the main discussions on campus was whether seminaries should be academic institutions that gave people a strong theological foundation, or training programs. For the most part, the academics won in my seminary as well as in most mainline seminaries. I've always found this argument to be a false one, though. Why can't seminaries be both? Why can't they ground people in a strong theology while also giving them practical skills? I may have been given a strong theological foundation, but I graduated from seminary with very little practical understanding of how to pastor a church. I had no idea how to run a board meeting, how to craft a vision, how to create cohesion, or how to resolve conflicts. For me, those skills came from my training as a counselor, social worker, and spiritual director. In this section I will offer some practical, pragmatic lessons I learned as a therapist and spiritual director in how to overcome dysfunctional patterns and to lead people to a unifying sense of health.

1. *To be a unifying leader means to be a nonanxious presence.* This concept comes from family therapy, and it is a crucial one not only for therapists but also for congregational leaders. In short, to be a nonanxious presence means to project calmness in all situations, especially crises. I learned the importance of becoming a nonanxious presence before becoming a pastor, and I learned it in a somewhat painful way. As part of my studies for my master of social work degree, I was working part-time doing fieldwork in a pastoral counseling agency. I was assigned to be the therapist for a young couple who had a history of violent arguments.

I had been working with them for several weeks when I experienced firsthand one of their fights. We were in the midst of exploring an issue when the husband told his wife that he really didn't like her. He was a very tall, thin man who held back his feelings and thoughts. She was a short, heavy, bombastic woman who rarely had an unexpressed emotion. When he said this to her, she jumped out of her seat, stormed across the room, and shouted in his face that he had wasted her life. He shrunk deeper into his chair, clenching his fists.

My insides roiled. I began to panic. I had no idea what to do, and I felt certain she was on the verge of hitting him. In a panicky voice I said to him, "H-h-how do you feel? I mean, what's this feel like to you? W-w-what do you feel inside?" He said, "I feel like killing her," as he stood up and towered over her. She stepped back, and I stood up, speaking quickly in a high-pitched voice: "N-n-n-now, let's all calm down." They both sat down, but I knew at that point that I had lost them as a therapist. They had no respect for me. I was inadequate, and they were stuck in their old patterns.

What was especially painful for me was that the whole session was on audiotape. (As part of my field education, I had to tape my counseling sessions and then share them with my supervisor.) Later that week my supervisor and I met, and he zeroed in on that segment of the session. "What's going on there? Do you realize that you've lost this couple?" I tried to defend myself, saying that I had said all the things I had been trained to say, but I knew he was right. He then proceeded to give me perhaps the best practical advice I've been given, not only about counseling, but also about leadership. He said, "Graham, to be an effective therapist, you have to be a nonanxious presence. You not only have to remain in control, but when all hell is breaking loose, you have to be the picture of calm, because it is your calm that will teach them that there is another way to get through their difficulties. If you lose your cool, you will be telling them that there is no hope, that even you can't find a way out. But if you remain calm and peacefully ask them to sit down, take a break and a breath, and then in a relaxed tone ask them to explore what just happened, you will give them the gift of insight."

He was right. The next week, as if on cue, they fought. She stormed over, and he shrunk back in his chair, clenching his fists. I said to her in as calm a voice as I could muster, "Let's take a step back right now and take a breath." They both looked at me as though I was crazy, but I insisted by calmly saying, "I need a break right now, so let's all take a break." She sat down and I very peaceably said to her, "I notice that this is the pattern you both have when he says what he really feels. You get angry and in his face." Turning to him, I said, "And you shrink down. Tell me what's going on." It was amazing. They remained calm and began to explore this dynamic between them. I was once again the therapist. I had their respect.

Too many leaders yell at their staff, their members, and the other leaders of the church. I remember a member telling me about her husband's experience in another church. He was the clerk of that church's board, and he refused to sign off on something the board had decided because he felt that the pastor had manipulated the board. The pastor erupted after the meeting. He proceeded to yell at the man, cursing him up and down. When the clerk turned his back and walked away, the pastor followed him all through the church, swearing at him, calling him selfish, ignorant, a failure, and "unsaved." That was the moment the pastor lost the church. The story quickly spread, and the church stopped responding. The pastor's temper brought division into the church.

Being a nonanxious presence means having the humility to remain calm in any situation and to project calmness, even if our insides are ready to explode. Even if we feel threatened and on the verge of losing control, we remain visibly calm. That doesn't mean that we remain unemotional. Instead, it means that we use our facial expressions, mannerisms, and body posture and language to bring tranquility to a situation. By remaining composed, and even slowing our interactions down, we reflect a sense of peacefulness and encourage others to move back to a calm center.

From a spiritual perspective, being a nonanxious presence means putting faith into action by trusting the Holy Spirit to restore peace and unity to the situation. Our calm becomes the centering action. In my own case, when I sense that emotions are getting raw, I will not only try to remain calm on the outside; often I will also halt discussions and invite people into a time of quiet. I'll say in a relaxed and somewhat soothing, deeper voice something along these lines: "I can tell we're getting a bit tired. Let's take a step back and center for a few moments. Let's just breathe and calm down. I'm going to spend a few moments in prayer just asking the Spirit to get us back on track, and I invite all of you to join me." After a minute or so of silence, I'll come back and say, "OK, this is what I just heard all of you say," and then I'll summarize the conversation to that point. Only then do I invite people back into discussion. Fortunately, I've not had to do this too often, but it has happened. The key is to become a nonanxious presence to others that actually allows us to embody Christ's presence, and to lead people back to being open to the Holy Spirit.

2. *To be a unifying leader means to have respect and positive regard for everyone, even the least person.* Showing this kind of respect can be difficult, especially with those we believe are resisting and perhaps even subverting our ministries. It is impossible to be perfect in our regard for others. There are just times when we slip and treat people with disrespect. This happens most often with the people who feel free to treat us with little or no respect. Still, there are practical ways to treat people with respect and to have a positive regard for them, even if they have little for us. First, there's a lesson that I've learned from watching my father. My father is a United States federal judge, a position that makes him a prestigious and powerful man. At the same time, I don't think I've ever seen him act on that prestige. He speaks in the same friendly and respectful way to everyone, from other judges to custodians.

For example, he is always grateful for whatever they do. He praises them for their work, telling them how great it was, even if what they did was a simple and small task. He is not afraid to be humble with them and to admit that he has no skill in whatever they do. And he doesn't do this for show. He does it because he is aware of his gifts and his limitations. He recognizes his abilities as a judge, but he also admits that he cannot unclog drains, do anything electrical, understand the workings of an engine, or serve food to others with a smile and grace. He treats others as though they are as important as he is, as he believes they are. This is what it means to treat others with respect and positive regard. It means recognizing our own limitations and having gratitude for what others have to offer, no matter how simple.

In the same way, we need to be respectful and to have positive regard for everyone if we are to be effectively humble leaders. I have a general rule of thumb: nothing that takes place in a church is so important that it is worth blowing up over and destroying relationships. That doesn't mean that I don't get angry. Instead, it means that I make sure that I remain focused on respecting the other even when I am angry. And in my interactions with others, I try to be as respectful as I can be, even if I truly disagree with another, or if he has disturbed or distressed me. That doesn't mean that others always experience my interactions that way. It simply means that I try as best I can to make them that way.

3. *To be a unifying leader means being a gentle and patient leader.* One of big problem in churches is that as leaders we are often in too much of a hurry to accomplish our vision. What we fail to realize is that our vision is not necessarily shared or even grasped by all others. If we are pastors, our vision generally emerges out of years of reflection, training, and experience (and sometimes even out of the workshop we attended last week). We then move into a church and can't understand why the lay leaders won't latch onto our vision right away. The answer is that for most of them, our vision is new, or at least it's articulated in a new way. Not all people understand and accept new visions at the same rate. So we have to be gentle leaders who are patient with our congregants, recognizing that implementing our vision can take time.

There's a general rule in education about how much new material can be introduced to a class: you can move a class only as fast as the slowest student. There's a lot of wisdom to this rule. It says that if we teach only those who grasp things easily, we leave other students in the dust. It may bore students who grasp things more quickly to go slow, but if I really care about all the students, then I will slow the lessons down enough to help the slowest student keep up with the rest of the class. I also can enlist the rest of the class in helping the slower student. I believe this rule applies to pastoral leadership. We can move only as fast as our slowest leader. So if someone on a board just doesn't "get" the vision, more time needs to be spent formulating and articulating the vision. We have to assume that this leader represents a significant proportion of members who also require a greater amount of time to get the picture. As pastoral leaders, we need to remember to be accommodating and to keep everyone on board. This task requires gentleness and patience.

4. *To be a unifying leader means to let humor lead people to humility.* I believe that humor is a huge part of being a church. Congregations that can't laugh together can't serve together because they are just too serious to truly find joy in serving God. I believe that humor and humility share a connection in that the best humor reminds us that not everything is as serious as we make it out to be. The best humor is earthy humor that pokes fun at pride and pretentiousness. If you consider what consistently makes most people laugh, it is poking fun at the very things that lead people away from humility. As a result, I find that even in the midst of the most serious discussion, finding a way to insert an absurd, comical, droll, or witty comment can relieve tensions and open us up to being more creative. Perhaps as a teen I was excessively influenced by the English comedy group Monty Python, but it is hard for me not to see an absurd side to any situation, even the most difficult ones. I find that sharing absurd observations often helps all of us to become more humble by pointing out our weaknesses in the presence of God, thereby allowing us to seek God's will better together. I find this to be true in meetings, counseling sessions, and worship. Humor can have a unifying effect for one simple reason: people who laugh together become closer, even if in small ways.

5. *To be a unifying leader means keeping a balance between care of self and care for a congregation.* Very simply, we cannot unify others if we are unable to create boundaries between our personal lives and our congregational lives. Developing these boundaries requires the formation of a fairly strong sense of self, a sense of personal integrity within as well as a strong sense of divine union with God. Developing a strong sense of self means being self-aware and aware of my limitations, as best I can. I must make time to work on my relationship with God while also understanding myself—my motivations and my habits, especially those that might cause me to succumb to Sacrifice Syndrome. Becoming self-aware means spending regular time in prayer and

creating a prayer discipline. It can also mean creating a personal rule for life.

Creating a rule for life may be one of the least applied spiritual disciplines of all, but it is a crucial one. What principles and ideals drive you as a leader? What activities will you or won't you engage in? What is the foundation of your life? Creating a rule helps us answer these questions.

The idea of creating a rule for life emerged out of the early monastic tradition of Christianity, specifically with Benedict of Nursia, who lived between 480 and 547 CE. Benedict was very much aware that the Roman culture was constantly being assaulted from within and without. During his lifetime, the Western Roman Empire, and especially the Italian peninsula, was under regular assault from barbarian tribes. Attacks on Rome and the surrounding provinces had been taking place for years, causing the culture to break down from without. At the same time, Roman culture had become completely self-indulgent. Vice was rampant, as was a hedonistic immorality. Benedict became concerned over the ease with which people could fall into despair, destruction, and overindulgence. His answer was to create a 73-point rule for the monks at the monastery at Monte Cassino. The rule was meant to guide the monks in the midst of an unstable culture filled with violence, temptations, and turmoil. Benedict's Rule was a practice that would teach adherents to embrace humility, obedience, balance, work, reflection, rest, and the general ordering of religious life.[10]

We don't have to become Benedictine monks to craft a rule. All it requires is sitting down and deciding how to order our own lives in our own context. When and how often will we pray? What activities will we consider to be essential? How will we determine what we are and are not called to do? What will our eating, exercising, and sleeping habits be? How will we strike a balance between home and work? The answers to these questions are found as we prayerfully seek God's guidance on the practical ways we should discipline our lives so that we live life as God intended us to live. A rule is a written statement delineating just how we will live. For instance, a rule might say,

1. Pray each day for 20 minutes.
2. Read Scripture for 30 minutes each evening before going to bed.
3. Treat all people in my interactions with respect.

A rule can be long or short. The point is that it be a reflection of the practical steps we believe God is leading us to take to discipline our lives so that we will live in alignment with God's will. When we form a strong sense of self and divine union with God, then we are able to lead from a strong center, which enables us to resist the pull of the many fads and fashions, and even traditions, that beckon us to serve them instead of God. We can become more adept at discerning God's will for our congregations. We can lead a church to enter into a divine union with Christ as we seek Christ's will together.

UNIFYING LEADERSHIP

To be a humble leader means to be a unifying leader. It means becoming self-aware and having integrity, while also becoming unified with God. It means overcoming a culture that is captured by the powers of division both within the church and outside it. It requires us, as leaders, to make relationships primary. We have to let go of generational, ideological, and cultural currents that divide us.

If we are to resist the dividing influences of the world around us, the most important thing we can do is to immerse ourselves in God. Unfortunately, in our present culture the lines are often blurred between what is of the culture and what is Christian. To some extent this blurring of lines has always been present but in different forms. Twenty years ago being a Christian in business or governmental leadership was discouraged. Today we face a different problem as Christian faith has become more acceptable and in some circles, such as politics, is now required of a candidate. Many Christian leaders, both in congregations and secular positions, resist the call to become humble. The primary symptom of that resistance is that few have the ability even to consider the possibility that "I may be wrong," that "what I believe may not be God's truth." To be a humble leader means not only to consider this possibility but to lead others to consider this possibility. The more we indulge people in division, the more we lead people away from God. I believe that the answer to divisiveness is humble prayer, and the more divided we are, the more we need to become immersed in prayer as a community and congregation.

Ultimately, as the body of Christ our churches are called to develop a sense of unity with each other, but we cannot develop this unity unless we are willing to be united with Christ as leaders. Leading a congregation to unity is perhaps the biggest challenge our churches face in the next 20 years.

Chapter 5

Spirit-Led Leadership

·+·≡◆≡·+·

If you love me, you will keep my commandments. And I will ask the Father, and he will give you another Advocate, to be with you forever. This is the Spirit of truth, whom the world cannot receive, because it neither sees him nor knows him. You know him, because he abides with you, and he will be in you.

John 14:15–17

BACK IN 1997 WE KNEW SOMETHING WAS COMING. BUT WE DIDN'T know what. We had been growing as a congregation for a few years, and we were running out of room. We needed more storage, classroom, and youth program space. The problem was that we weren't quite sure what to do about it all.

When I first came to Calvin Presbyterian Church to be its pastor, some fairly serious issues with the building needed to be dealt with—issues that made it difficult for me to agree to become the pastor. The church was worn down. It had last been renovated in 1954, and since then very little had been taken care of physically other than the fellowship hall and kitchen, which had been redone cosmetically. It wasn't the congregation's fault. The church had been in decline for more than 30 years. They had gone from a high of about 380 members in 1965 to about 215 members when I came. During that time, they had to cut budgets and struggled to determine what was or wasn't an economic priority. They faced the same dilemmas that most of our mainline congregations face today, which is how to support ministry in an aging building, one that requires increased funding to maintain. By the time I came to Calvin Church, the building was in very poor shape. The sanctuary was dingy, with wrinkling carpet that had been pulling up from the floor for years and could no longer be stretched to fit the floor. Everything in the sanctuary was either dark brown or a deep shade of red, making for a worship space that seemed tired and old. In the church library, red flocking wallpaper was peeling off the walls. The primary colors of all the classrooms were dark brown and burnt orange. In the downstairs classroom, a heavy tarp that acted as a classroom divider sagged from its ceiling track. After I visited the church building for the first time, I drove away teary-eyed. I loved what I had seen of the people of the church, but I sensed that I could spend my whole career there renovating a building in disrepair. This was not something I wanted to do in my ministry. In the end, though, I sensed God calling me to this church despite my reluctance.

Three years after I had become Calvin Church's pastor, changes had been made. We had begun to grow and to receive new members. We had renovated the sanctuary, making it brighter and more vibrant while also retaining its traditional charm. But we knew there was more to be done, and we didn't know what to do. We were left in a quandary: do we build on, build up, or build out? As part of a three-year capital campaign, we had left undesignated the funds to be raised during the second year of our campaign—the one devoted to creating more ministry space. We decided to wait and see what God would lead us to do. Waiting is hard for any congregation to do. We wanted to figure out our options and to develop a definite plan. Instead, we were waiting, seeking, praying, and trying to discern God's plan.

In the midst of waiting, we decided to consult with an architect to determine what sorts of actions we would need to take if we kept growing at our current pace. The architect told us that either we had to buy new property, at least 17 acres, and move, or we had to buy the three lots with houses on them adjoining the church. He encouraged us to move. We discussed these possibilities within the church, and in the end we were clear that God was calling us to remain where we were. Then God acted. Immediately upon discerning that we were called to remain where we were, we discovered that the first of the three houses targeted by the architect was for sale, and in fact, its asking price had been reduced by $10,000 that week. We acted quickly.

We called a meeting of the session to discern whether God was calling us to buy this house. We toured the house and then spent more time in prayer. We struggled with the practicalities: should we spend money on the house, or save our money for other eventualities? Some session members who had previously had bad experiences in declining churches cautioned us against buying the house. One commented that in her mother's church, a young pastor had persuaded the church to engage in a capital campaign and then departed, leaving the church with a crushing debt. It didn't matter that I had no intentions of leaving in the middle of a campaign. This elder believed that pastors couldn't be trusted in such matters. Eventually, we were able to put aside our more practical concerns and pray. We sought God's will, and it became apparent that God was calling us to buy the house, using money from the sale of the church manse several years earlier as well as money collected as part of our capital campaign.

Buying this house became one of the greatest gifts that this church had ever experienced. We called it "Faith House" because we believed it reflected our faith that God would reveal a path for us—and God did. Over the ensuing three years, we ended up buying the other two properties the architect had targeted for us; and as I write, we are in a second capital campaign to build more classrooms as well as office space.

Our leadership's willingness to recognize that something might be coming, and to wait and prepare for it, was essential to the health of Calvin Church because it created the opportunity for growth by removing obstacles. The church leadership was willing to look and plan ahead while remaining open to God's possibilities, to the power of the Holy Spirit. What the leadership of Calvin Church did was not easy by any stretch of the imagination because it meant moving in two directions at the same time. On the one hand, the leaders had to be proactive, planning for growth. On the other hand, the leaders had to be willing to wait, pray, and discern.

Too often leaders and churches are not very open to the power of the Holy Spirit and the leadings of Christ. Many churches and leaders are reactive, waiting until a problem arises before trying to figure out a solution or a strategy. They get caught up in a crisis-management approach that consists of waiting until they are fully ensconced in a crisis, or on the verge of one, and then try to figure out how to deal with it. Their solutions are rarely God-inspired. Instead, their decisions could be characterized as either grasping at straws or doing what they've always done, thinking that if they just work harder and better, what they've always done will eventually work.

The more effective leaders and churches act *proactively*, scanning the horizon to anticipate potential problems or possibilities and then creating elaborate plans and processes to deal with them. They develop one-, three-, five-, and even ten-year strategic plans, complete with goals and strategies to accomplish them. Unfortunately, no matter how proactive they are, they can never get quite enough information, understand their situation well enough, or foresee events clearly enough to prepare for all eventualities. They fail to take into account all sorts of demographic, sociological, generational, and religious trends that can hit like a tornado, ripping apart churches and their plans.

The problem with both reactive and proactive approaches is that the world is changing so quickly and dramatically that it leaves reactive leaders feeling overwhelmed by the constant problems they face in their churches and surrounding cultures, and makes proactive leaders feel like failures because they can never gauge the church and the surrounding culture accurately. Reactive leaders constantly face a world they cannot understand and react to properly, while proactive leaders try to understand the world but eventually get overwhelmed with information and struggle to determine which information is relevant in the face of a constantly shifting culture.

For example, in the two decades that I have been ordained, the church and the surrounding culture have changed dramatically. Contemporary worship was just a whisper at the time of my ordination, something that Pentecostals and strange churches did—at least that's what we thought. Churches were declining, but few adequate theories were advanced to explain why. The opinions of young pastors like me were mostly ignored because we were seen as inexperienced and therefore inadequately prepared to address the decline in a local congregation. The prevailing notion was that people my age would return to church once we began having children. The worship wars were just beginning, and members of the G.I. generation were still firmly in charge of churches.

In 1991, the Presbyterian Church (U.S.A.), amid great fanfare, introduced a brand-new hymnal. The committee that put it together had done a marvelous job of soliciting opinions of Presbyterian worshipers all around the country, seeking to include hymns that were beloved. A majority of Presbyterian churches eventually bought the hymnals. Unfortunately, a major flaw soon became apparent to some: nonworshipers and younger Christians hadn't been consulted. To those of us who were younger, the hymnal's emphasis on traditional and classical hymns left us thinking that the hullabaloo over the new hymnal was much ado about nothing. The music was still the music many of us had rejected, or at least had relegated to being "our parents' music," and therefore being irrelevant to our generation. No one seemed to care what music might attract those outside the church, let alone put that music in the new hymnal. For those of us who were younger at the time, it was quickly apparent that the church really didn't factor us into the equation. As the decline of the PCUSA began to hit crisis mode, the leadership of the denomination and local churches grappled to attract younger adults. We still do.

Many churches began to offer contemporary services, some of which did attract younger worshipers, but offering these services didn't work for everyone. Many churches *reacted* to the problems as their pastors and leaders grasped at straws, seeking any program that would halt the decline. Others tried to act proactively by making elaborate plans to attract members, often failing because they simply didn't know what would attract young adults. They lacked not only good information about what to do, but proper strategies. The result? In the PCUSA, along with other mainline denominations, the decline has continued at the same pace. Why?

Probably the best description of the reason has come from Bill Easum in his book *Leadership on the OtherSide*.[1] His analysis is that our culture and our churches are caught in a wormhole. The idea of wormholes is a staple of science fiction and astrophysics. It is a theoretical, twisting, tunnel-like connection between two distinct and distant parts of the universe. The theory of wormholes is based on the idea that space is not expansive like the interior of a ball. Rather, it is flat and crumpled like a piece of paper, with the galaxies resting on the surface of the great, crumpled plane. To go from one point in the galaxy to another might take millions of light years traveling along the plane of the universe, but a wormhole could get you there in a fraction of the time (assuming you could travel at the speed of light). Wormholes connect two points on the crumpled plane, points that may be distant following the surface of the plane, but may be close together between the crumples. For example, the first word on a page may be far physically from the last word, but if you crumple the paper into a ball, they can become quite close and even touch. A wormhole plunges through the emptiness between the crumples to connect distant points on a plane, yet that may be close if the universe (as many physicists theorize) is like a crumpled paper ball.

Hypothetically a spaceship entering a wormhole in our galaxy could exit into a whole new galaxy, a galaxy vastly different from our own—perhaps one that is billions of years older than our own and thus more developed. Acclimated to our own galaxy, we would enter the wormhole and exit into a galaxy whose very fabric was different and difficult to understand. This is the realm of church today. We are leaving an age of Christendom in which the rules for church, religion, and faith were fairly well known and accepted. We are moving toward a new realm of life and faith, one that also has certain rules and requirements. The problem is that because we are not there yet, we do not know what to expect. The most expert proactive leadership can be rendered moot in an instant, because this new realm works according to rules and laws that are only slowly becoming understood. As Easum says:

> You and I are part of a something big. Our world is plunging head over heels through a remarkable period of history. The epistemological, philosophical, ontological, and metaphysical structures underlying all of our belief and values systems

are coming apart and being reassembled. As a result, the way people process knowledge is undergoing a profound metamorphosis of mind and heart. Something of this magnitude happens only once or twice a millennium.

This change of mind and heart is occurring so rapidly and relentlessly that many of today's leaders are paralyzed with fright. Their hearts can't take the ride, so they're resigned to a slow, agonizing death of spirit. Such fear among church leaders has never been experienced before, not even while some of our predecessors burned at the stake.[2]

While I think Easum may be guilty of hyperbole in the last paragraph, especially with his suggestion that church leaders have *never* experienced this degree of sudden change before, I think his overall point is valid. The changes occurring today are rapid, and they do create anxiety among mainline church leaders. Also, they require the development of new approaches to congregational life—some of which renew old rituals and some of which create new rituals. Ultimately, Easum's point is important. He tells us that we are in something akin to a wormhole that leads the traveler away from a comfortable and familiar realm of understanding that is no longer adequate for a world that is changing. It leads to a new realm of understanding that is not yet clear and whose rules are not easily ascertained. As leaders of congregations in the wormhole, we are responsible for leading the church through a time of transition in which the old ways no longer make sense and the new ways are not yet clear. The church needs a kind of leadership that is able to anticipate the future while simultaneously discerning God's path for getting there. This leadership cannot be dominated by fear and uncertainty but instead must lead in faith toward a direction that is discerned as much as it is planned for. As Easum says:

Effective leaders today reside somewhere between absolute order and absolute chaos. The trick is to ride the wave of chaos to its crest without becoming engulfed by it. Instead of seeking order, leaders court chaos. The worst thing a leader can do today is avoid the chaos of the moment for the order of the past. To do so signs one's death warrant as a leader and consigns the organization to death.[3]

So what kind of leadership are we talking about? It is one that isn't quite reactive, yet it recognizes that sometimes it is impossible not to be reactive. It is leadership that tries to be proactive but recognizes that the future is glimpsed more than it is grasped because of the wormhole nature of the future we are traveling toward. It is proactive but also flexible, willing to jettison plans and strategies when faced with the reality that God may have other plans. This leadership integrates the best of both reactive and proactive leadership but also enables church leaders to move in God's direction. This leadership is *Spirit-active* leadership. But before we explore what Spirit-active leadership is, let's discuss a bit more in depth reactive and proactive leadership, including their shortcomings.

From Reactive to Proactive Leadership

While the term "proactive" had been circulating in management literature throughout the early and mid-1980s, it was really business management guru Stephen R. Covey who made it part of our culture's lexicon through his book *The Seven Habits of Highly Effective People*. Covey wrote about the need for business managers and leaders to become proactive rather than reactive. His insights on developing the habit of proactivity emerged from the writings of the Austrian psychiatrist and Auschwitz concentration camp survivor Victor Frankl. In the concentration camp, Frankl discovered that he had a freedom that could not be killed by the Nazis, no matter what they did to his body. He had the freedom to choose how he would respond to his situation. Frankl realized that some people are trapped in a belief that they have no choice; that they must simply react to the uncontrollable situations swirling around them. They feel as though their lives and situations are determined by fate, and so they have no freedom.

They are stuck in a predetermined dance, like puppets controlled by a great puppet master.

Frankl recognized that those who died quickly from the conditions of the camp were generally those who believed they had lost all freedom to choose and fell into despair. They were reactive. As Covey says:

> Reactive people are often affected by their physical environment. If the weather is good, they feel good. If it isn't, it affects their attitude and their performance. Proactive people can carry their own weather with them. . . . They are value driven; and if their value is to produce good quality work, it isn't a function of whether the weather is conducive to it or not.[4]

In contrast to those who sensed they had no freedom, some maintained a sense of dignity and purpose that seemed to help them survive. Certainly many of these people died, too, but they were able to recognize that even their looming physical death didn't take away their choice of how to face death. These were the proactives.

Covey took this idea of freedom of choice, even in the face of devastation, and applied it to business leadership. He pointed out that business leaders can take charge of their situations and refuse to succumb to the environment. Instead, they can look for ways to plough through and cultivate something good, even in the worst situations.

For him, reactive leaders use such phrases as, "There's nothing I can do. That's just the way I am. He makes me so mad. They won't allow that. I have to do that."[5] Similar phrases are often spoken by church leaders and pastors. They face declining congregations and say, "The congregation simply won't follow. We've never done it this way before. The members of this church are resisting and subverting me. I have no choice but to do what they want."

In contrast, proactive leaders utter such phrases as "Let's look at our alternatives. I can choose a different approach. I control my own feelings. I can create an effective presentation. I will choose an appropriate response."[6] The proactive church leader or pastor uses similar phrases: "Let's consider this possibility. Let's try a different program. We can make this work."

Reactive leaders are also somewhat insular. They tend to focus attention on the things they know for certain that they can control, and that's what gets most of their attention. So the reactive leader tends to keep his sphere of attention on activities, relationships, and events that are in within what Covey calls the "Circle of Concern," a boundary that separates those things in which we have no "particular mental or emotional involvement" from those that draw our attention.[7] For instance, the Circle of Concern for a pastor might be the life of the church and surrounding community, as she generally ignores events beyond these, such as national or international issues. The reactive leader only fleetingly recognizes much of life beyond this circle. Remaining within the Circle of Concern, the reactive leader restricts her work even further to a much smaller "Circle of Influence." The Circle of Influence is the circle of people, situations, and events that she can influence, and maybe even control, for sure.[8]

For instance, reactive pastors may believe that they cannot control or influence the larger Circle of Concern, which would be the culture of the church, but, by golly, they can control the office, how it looks and how it operates, which is their Circle of Influence. Because they do not focus organizationally and operationally on problems and conditions outside of the small Circle of Influence, reactive leaders often lead organizations nowhere, since they can't get their focus off their immediate concerns—in this case the office and its operations. They are not able to consider possibilities beyond those presented by their Circle of Influence; as a result, potential problems often swirl around them in the larger Circle of Concern. But like ostriches, they keep their heads planted in their smaller Circle of Influence. Unable to deal with these difficulties, they let them fester and grow until these troubles eventually intrude into their Circle of Influence, creating a crisis.

While their operational and organizational focus may be the Circle of Influence, reactive leaders still obsess over their Circle of Concern. They obsess about "the weakness of other people, the problems in the environment, and circumstances over which they have no control."[9] In short, they operate in the realm of their influence but obsess about larger concerns and how these prevent them from being able to be more effective and have more influence.

Proactive leaders are also concerned about their circles of Concern and Influence, but they respond to them differently. While proactive leaders attempt to manage a well-defined Circle of Influence, they are always trying to expand their Circle of Influence so that it grows ever greater within the larger Circle of Concern. While reactive leaders feel helpless beyond their Circle of Influence, and thus tend to hide from problems until they are too large to ignore, proactive leaders try to enlarge their Circle of Influence, hoping that eventually their circles of Influence and Concern become almost the same. The point is that proactive leaders seek to expand their influence by anticipating problems, while reactive leaders hide from problems. Proactive leaders, as Covey says, "work on the things they can do something about. The nature of their energy is positive, enlarging, magnifying, causing their Circle of Influence to increase."[10] The result is that over time proactive leaders bring an organization to have a greater and greater influence on the community and world around it. Meanwhile, because reactive leaders cannot focus on anything but what little they can influence, their Circle of Influence and that of the organization they lead shrink over time. Summing up the theory of proactivity, Covey says, "We are responsible for our own effectiveness, for our own happiness, and ultimately, I would say, for most of our circumstances."[11]

The concepts of reactive and proactive leadership tell us a lot about the problems in the church today. Much of mainline denominational leadership has been reactive. Church laity, pastors, and denominational leaders feel trapped by a large Circle of Concern composed of cultural conditions that seem like a large moat surrounding them, preventing them from leaving their castles (and many of today's churches are like decaying castles— old buildings that once housed thriving congregations but now house increasingly trivial fiefdoms). They talk the language of proactivity, but they are trapped in reactivity. They feel trapped in a too rapidly changing world, and their few failed attempts to do something new have taught them that they are hopelessly consigned to their fate: to diminish until, at some far-off future date, they must accept the inevitable death that awaits their congregations and maybe even their denominations.

I look at my own denomination and see much reactive leadership. We talk about change, transformation, and renewal, but in the end we keep shrinking and becoming more and more insular as we pick intra-church fights with one another for not being the kinds of Christians and congregations we demand each other to be. Our Circle of Influence shrinks, because fewer of us are left in the denomination to influence. And our cultural influence has diminished to the point that we have very little cultural or political influence. This is in stark contrast to how much Presbyterians influenced American society for its first 200 years. For example, 11 of the 39 signers of the Declaration of Independence were Presbyterians. Twenty-five percent of our first 28 presidents were Presbyterian. Presbyterians were prominent leaders in all aspects of political, corporate, and religious life.

At the same time, I look at many leaders in nondenominational congregations and see proactive leadership. These congregations and their leaders refuse to accept the limits we easily accept in the mainline church. Their buildings do not look like ours, their music is not like ours, their staff and leadership structures are not like ours, their ministry is not like ours, and their mission is not like ours. That does not mean that we should copy them. It only means that they have been willing to be proactive while we remain stuck in a cycle of reactivity, pretending that we are proactive.

I want to be clear, though, that I do not believe that the salvation of the mainline church lies in copying the proactivity of the megachurch movement. I believe that our salvation will come as we adopt an approach to leadership that takes us a step beyond proactive leadership. I believe renewal will truly happen when we adopt a style of leadership I call "Spirit-active" leadership.

From Proactive to Spirit-Active Leadership

Proactive leadership has one major flaw, a defect that is not as evident in the business world as it is in the church world: proactive leadership is, by and large, *functional leadership.* It is leadership that cuts out the spiritual, and therefore the Spirit. Proactive leadership complies with human will. It tries to grow the Circle of Influence using functional, human insights, skills, and attributes. I am not saying that these are bad things. Proactive leadership fosters much that is good. But proactive leadership is still limited and limiting because it is the product of something I called "rational functionalism" in my book *Becoming a Blessed Church.* Rational functionalism is

> the tendency for denominations, their churches, and their leaders to subscribe to a view of faith and church that is overly rooted in a restrictive, logic-bound theology that ignores the possibility of spiritual experiences and miraculous events, while simultaneously overemphasizing functional practice that has become disconnected from an emphasis on leading people to a transforming experience of God.[12]

No matter how healthy proactive leadership is, it relies on human powers and skills to anticipate, plan, organize, and program. All forms of functional leadership, including proactive leadership, cut off the spiritual dimension so that God becomes less and less a part of our planning and decision making. We end up focusing our efforts on achieving our ambitions, never asking whether this is what God really wants.

I've seen how proactive leadership can lead to numerical growth but at the same time somehow diminish spiritual growth. Many members of our church became aware of the difference between a spiritual approach to faith and a more functional approach on a recent Good Friday. As a way of trying to spiritually deepen the Holy Week, Good Friday, and Easter Sunday experience, we invited all the members of our church to 24 hours of fasting and prayer, beginning after the Maundy Thursday

worship service and ending after the evening Good Friday worship service. To help them keep the fast on Good Friday, we offered a small service of prayer and reflection at lunchtime that
day. The point of this practice was to deepen their sense of reverence for Christ and the crucifixion.

While we were engaging in our time of prayer and fasting, we
became aware how differently a very large, nondenominational
church in the area approached Good Friday. That congregation
advertised to the community a Good Friday Easter egg hunt,
with over 4,400 Easter eggs, during which the church would raffle off free televisions. As one of our members said to me, "Let's
see, . . . We fast, and they give away free televisions. . . . There's
something funny going on here."

It's hard not to look at the Easter egg hunt and wonder where
the Spirit went. I understand what the leaders of the nondenominational church were trying to do, and I don't discount it. They
were trying to reach out to seekers and the unchurched, and
certainly many, many more attended their Easter egg hunt than
participated in our fast. Still, from the outside looking in, the decision to host a Good Friday Easter egg hunt and to raffle free
televisions seems very functional. It may be effective in attract-
ing visitors, but what is the spiritual impact? Was the decision
based on human ambition or the Spirit's guidance? The whole
point was to attract large numbers to the church, but was the
decision to host this event Spirit-led? Events can be successful
and attractive, yet still be functional and bar the Spirit. From the
outside looking in, I would say that their decision was proactive,
trying to expand their Circle of Influence, which is good for that
church. But the decision seemed also to be missing a spiritual
component—a question asking whether this promotional event
would lead people to an encounter with Christ, or if it would
merely attract attention. What would be the difference if Wal-
Mart had hosted an Easter egg hunt and raffled televisions? The
central question needs to be "Is this something God is calling us
to do?" Spirit-active leadership puts that question at the center,
not other questions, such as "Will this expand our Circle of Influence? Will this grow our church? Will this make us the preeminent church in the area, and maybe even the region?"

I would never advocate that a church leader not take advantage of a proactive style of leadership. It is a much healthier way of leading than reactive leadership. What I do advocate is placing at our center a style of leadership that does more than expand our Circle of Influence; one that seeks God's way, so that we can be led to discover whatever possibilities and opportunities God offers.

What is *Spirit-active* leadership? It is leadership that proactively considers all possibilities yet that does so by placing them before God in prayer. At its root it is humble leadership because it seeks God's way over our own way. As Spirit-active leaders, we prayerfully allow ourselves to be led by the Spirit to consider all possibilities and even to consider those that seem preposterous. The key is not the soundness of the idea but the extent to which we sense God's hand—providence—guiding us to a possible course of action, while it also seems to make the way clear for that action to occur. In other words, Spirit-active leaders are always looking for the window that God opens for us whenever a door before us is closed.

Spirit-active leaders are providential leaders, relying on and expecting divine coincidences as a regular part of ministry and mission. I believe that this very facet of Spirit-active leadership is the aspect that is most difficult because it takes a portion of leadership out of our hands and puts it in the hands of God, whom we never really see or understand. It requires a tremendous amount of trust in the power of the Holy Spirit, yet, to put it bluntly, most of us have a hard time trusting anyone, let alone God. What happens if we trust in God and God doesn't come through? What happens if we trust in divine providence and nothing happens? What if we experience what we think is a divine coincidence, and it turns out to be a mirage?

We recently struggled with the tension between being proactive and Spirit-active in our church session. As I mentioned previously, we are in the midst of a capital campaign preparing to build a $1.4 million addition onto the church for offices and classrooms, and in the process we have been considering whether to temporarily move our Sunday school classes as well as the nursery school that rents space from us to an adjacent house that the church owns. We have to do something since we will lose the use of most of our classrooms and the fellowship hall for over seven months. Do we need to bring the house up to code for the nursery school, and if we do, how much will it cost? What do we need to do to prepare the house for our classes? How will we make up the lost revenue from the rent of the house? What are the alternatives?

The questions paralyzed us for a few months as we sifted through a multitude of options, none of which was optimal. Each option created some sort of financial drain and logistical problems. It was difficult to discern God's will because there were just too many "what ifs": What if we do this but the loss of rent on one of the houses puts us in financial difficulty? What if we rent a trailer to put classes in; what will the cost be and how will it impact us financially? What will happen to our education program if we do this, since we are asking people to walk outside in the winter to a house a block away? What will happen to the nursery school that operates within our church?

In my mind, moving into the house seemed obvious, but it didn't seem so to others who were concerned about the financial implications. Amid all the "what ifs," we spent time talking about what it means to prayerfully discern God's will and follow faithfully in God's direction. I suggested that the session members take more time in prayer to consider what God wants, and to try, as best as they could, to put aside all the "what ifs." Then divine providence took over. The nursery school that rented space from us discovered an opportunity to move to another church for a year. The tenants who were renting our house had an opportunity to buy their own house and had entered into an agreement on it. They wanted to be let out of their contract several months early, about the time we would need to move into the house. Even though our session was paralyzed with "what ifs," it was apparent that God was moving forward anyway, and we were left with a choice: remain paralyzed, or jump on the ship and follow the flow. After spending time in prayer, we jumped on the ship and decided to move forward and to prepare the house for classes in the fall. As Spirit-active leaders, we not only sought divine providence, but we embraced it.

In essence, Spirit-active leadership requires surrender and reliance upon God. I don't mean a kind of helpless surrender, but a surrender of will to seek a single will—the union of our will with God's will. The best way to describe this surrender is to say that we seek to enter a state of "willingness." Too often people are either willful or will-less. To be willful means to be narcissistic and egotistic, always seeking to make our will, what we want, dominant. When we are willful, all that matters to us is that we get our way. In the workplace, we always seek control and advantage. In relationships we always seek dominance—to be the alpha dog. In social situations, we want to be the center.

To be will-less means to have little will of our own and to seek to have people around us who have a strong enough will to tell us what to do and how to live. We lack confidence in our own decisions and define ourselves through others' eyes. We fear being alone or on our own because we need others to care for us.

To be willing means to let go of our will and to seek only God's will (if we tend to be willful), or to build up our will and give it to God in service (if we are will-less). One way or another, to be willing means to unite our will with God's will so that we *will* one will: God's. Ultimately, that is what Spirit-active leadership is. It seeks God's will in everything and so looks for God's guidance, possibilities, and opportunities in everything.

MYSTICAL INTELLIGENCE

In a lot of ways, being a Spirit-active leader is much like being open to "the Force." You know what the Force is. It is the religious, spiritual power found in the *Star Wars* films. It is a power that those following the Jedi faith say surrounds us, fills us, flows through us, that both controls our actions and responds to them. It is what gives the Jedi Knight his or her power.

There's a scene in one of the *Star Wars* films, *The Empire Strikes Back*, that really reflects much of the idea of the roots of Spirit-active leadership. In the scene, the Jedi Master, Yoda, is training Luke Skywalker to be a Jedi Knight. Skywalker is upside down, standing on one hand, with Yoda standing on the sole of one of his feet. At the same time, Skywalker uses his mind to levitate several boxes and rocks. As this is going on, Yoda explains the Force to him. Suddenly his spaceship, which is submerged half-way in a swamp, sinks even more. That movement causes Sky-walker to lose his concentration, and as he does, everything falls to the ground, including him.

Walking to the edge of the swamp, he complains that he will never get the spaceship out. Yoda suggests that Skywalker use the Force to get it out. Petulantly, Skywalker says to Yoda that using the Force to suspend rocks in the air is one thing, but using the Force to lift a spaceship out of a swamp is something entirely different. Yoda becomes irritated, saying, "No! No different!" Skywalker says, "All right. I'll give it a try." Yoda says, "No! Try not. Do, or do not! There is no try."

Skywalker, a bit skeptical, stands at the edge of the swamp, closes his eyes, and focuses with his hand outstretched. As he does, the water begins to bubble. The spaceship slowly lifts, and Yoda's eyes widen. Then it's over. The ship slips back even deep-er into the water. Skywalker walks over to Yoda, sits, and breath-ing heavily says, "I can't. It's too big."

Yoda looks at Skywalker and says, "Size matters not. Look at me. Judge me by my size, will you? And well you should not. For my ally is the force. And a powerful ally it is. Life breeds it; makes it grow. Its energy surrounds and binds us. Luminous beings are we, not this crude matter. You must feel the Force around you." How does Skywalker respond? He says to Yoda, "You want the impossible!"

Yoda, looking disappointed, stands, closes his eyes, and stretches his hand out as he concentrates. The water again bub-bles. The ship slowly lifts, higher and higher. Eventually the ship rises out of the water and moves over the water, toward the land. Skywalker steps out of the way as the ship gently touches down on the ground before him. He walks up to the ship, looking in disbelief as he feels its hull. He then walks over to Yoda and says, "I don't . . . I don't believe it." Yoda, in a calm voice, replies, "That is why you fail."[13]

There's so much in that scene that speaks to Christian life, and especially to Spirit-active leadership. I don't want somehow to give you the impression that my faith is in the Force, or that I somehow think that *Star Wars* is a real religion. But it does offer a metaphor for a way of grace-filled life that we often forget is a part of the Christian life, a way that can be a major foundation of Christian leadership. There's a reason why the idea of the "the Force" had so much resonance in the American culture when the *Star Wars* films came out, and why it still resonates. It resonates because there's something Christian about the idea of the Force, especially in terms of our understanding of power of the Holy Spirit. Embedded in the idea of the Force and Christianity is the idea that there is a mystical force that can influence events and open us to possibilities.

There is a power that starts with God but that can flow through all of life, not only binding us in love but giving us divine power. Jesus suggested as much when he said, "Truly I tell you, if you have faith and do not doubt, not only will you do what has been done to the fig tree, but even if you say to this mountain, 'Be lifted up and thrown into the sea,' it will be done" (Matt. 21:21).

St. Patrick of Ireland understood this idea of grace flowing around, in, and through us. Over 1500 years ago he is reported to have written a now-famous prayer that expressed the idea that Christ and God's grace are everywhere. He wrote:

> Christ be with me, Christ within me,
> Christ behind me, Christ before me,
> Christ beside me, Christ to win me,
> Christ to comfort and restore me,
> Christ beneath me, Christ above me,
> Christ in quiet, Christ in danger,
> Christ in hearts of all that love me,
> Christ in mouth of friend and stranger.[14]

This prayer is saying that Christ and Christ's grace are everywhere, and that if we live in him, his grace will live in us. To become open to this reality, we need to develop a sense of *mystical intelligence*, which is what St. Patrick had. What is mystical intelligence? It's similar in nature to intellectual intelligence, as measured by IQ, and something called *emotional intelligence*.

Intellectual intelligence should be fairly familiar. It is our level of intellectual aptitude, our ability to grasp cognitively the world around us. To test intelligence, we use IQ tests, which measure a person's reasoning and problem-solving ability. In contrast, emotional intelligence (EI) has to do with the awareness a person has of herself and others. As Richard Boyatzis and Annie McKee write in their book *Resonant Leadership:*

> EI includes four domains: self-awareness, self-management, social awareness, and relationship management. The first two domains determine how well we understand and manage ourselves and our emotions; the latter two dictate how well we recognize and manage the emotions of others, build relationships, and work in complex social systems.[15]

I believe that there is another level of intelligence, a deeper level of intelligence. This is mystical intelligence, which has to do with how aware we are of God's purpose, presence, and power. Mystical intelligence is more of an intuitive, transcendent ability than either intellectual or emotional intelligence. Like the Jedis using the Force, we become aware of mystical, grace-filled power wherever we are. It's an aptitude. Some people seem to have it to a greater degree than others, or at least they've worked to develop it more than others, but it's something that all Christians, especially Christian leaders, need.

Essentially three elements constitute mystical intelligence. Much of what we have already spoken about both in this and earlier chapters contributes to mystical intelligence—factors such as humility, prayerfulness, faith, self-awareness, openness, Spirit-activeness, and much more. Still, some factors are specific to mystical intelligence itself. The following are the three elements.

1. *An intuitive, integrative awareness of God's presence in all situations.* Mystical intelligence begins with cultivating a deep awareness of God's presence in all situations. To me it sounds obvious to say that God is in every situation and that God's presence can be sensed everywhere, but I don't think it is evident to many Christians. In fact, while many or most Christians grow up being taught that God is omnipresent, they don't necessarily make the

connection in their minds that if God is omnipresent, then God must be present in every situation and have an impact on every situation, an impact that can be sensed. To many Christians, God's omnipresence is an abstract idea that is hard to bring into everyday life. There may be moments when they are aware that God permeates everything, but often they live life as though God is only minimally present. Part of the problem is that they miss what Christian mystics have always understood, the practical impact of omnipresence. As 18th-century Roman Catholic mystic Jean-Pierre de Caussade said in correspondence with a woman who was struggling to find God in her life:

> You are seeking God, dear sister, and he is everywhere. Everything proclaims him to you, everything reveals him to you, everything brings him to you. He is by your side, over you, around and in you. Here he is dwelling and yet you still seek him. Ah! You are searching for God, the idea of God in his essential being. You seek perfection and it lies in everything that happens to you—your suffering, your actions, your impulses are the mysteries under which God reveals himself to you. But he will never disclose himself in the shape of that exalted image to which you so vainly cling.[16]

De Caussade had a tremendous belief and faith not only that God was present everywhere, but that the only thing preventing us from discovering God's purpose, presence, and power is our obstinate belief that somehow God isn't present. We may not believe explicitly that God isn't present, but we often do believe it implicitly. What's the difference? *Explicit belief* is what we tell people we believe—what we have learned we *should* believe. Explicit belief is what we *think* we believe, or what we've convinced ourselves that we believe, although our behaviors and deeply held biases may reveal a different belief. Explicit beliefs are our conscious beliefs. In best-case scenarios, implicit and explicit beliefs are the same. In most lives, though, there is a disconnection between the two.

Implicit belief is what we show we believe through our actions. Often our implicit beliefs are so deeply embedded that we aren't even aware they *are* our beliefs. So, while outwardly and explicitly we might say we believe in love, our actions may reveal an implicit lack of compassion and love for others. We might talk about love, but deep down we feel indifference towards others. I think the discrepancy between our explicit and implicit beliefs accounts for people's readiness to brand Christians as hypocrites. Often what we cognitively believe does not penetrate to the level of the heart and soul. The result is that we live divided lives, attesting to a great love of God and others on the outside, while remaining much more narcissistic and uncaring on the inside.

This same split between explicit and implicit beliefs affects the depth of our mystical intelligence. While we may explicitly say that we believe God is everywhere, our actions often show an implicit obliviousness to God everywhere. It becomes most apparent whenever we treat God, through our actions, as distant and removed from life—demonstrating beliefs much like those of the Deists (as some Deists are reported to have said, "God wound the first clock, God ticked the first tock, and then went on sabbatical leave"). When we do this, we see ourselves as being God's agents, working on behalf of a God who has gone away. I believe that far too many of our church leaders, and especially pastors, act as though they are agents for God, rather than conduits for God's Spirit, demonstrating their true implicit belief. They say God is everywhere, but in fact they act as though God has abdicated an active role in the world, sending agents instead, and that pastors and church leaders are those agents. As a result, they minister, but not from a deep foundation in prayer and awareness of God's presence. They may be theologically adept, trained in administration, and aware of the dynamics of congregational life, and perhaps even aware of certain spiritual practices, but they are ignorant of God's presence and voice all around us.

Mystical intelligence requires both an explicit and an implicit belief in God's presence—an integration of the two. Those with mystical intelligence not only believe that God is a deep presence, but they also have faith that God is always present and both directly and indirectly affecting whatever situation we are in. We believe that God cares deeply about what is taking place and that God will guide us to whatever outcome God wants for us.

Further, we believe that we can work with God and prayerfully influence how God acts in a situation, much in the way Abraham seemed to influence God when God planned to destroy Sodom (Gen. 18:22–33). Abraham pleaded for the righteous of the city of Sodom, finally persuading God not to destroy it so long as there were 10 righteous people in the city. (I have to assume that 10 couldn't be found because in the end the city was destroyed.) Those with mystical intelligence have a faith that they can influence God's decisions, but not in a capricious way. In the end, the only influence we have is to ask God to move in a way that is consistent with God's will for all creation. People with mystical intelligence want to act in consonance with God's eternal plan, which is filled with love, compassion, and justice.

Those with a deep sense of mystical intelligence would say that God is present in every situation and that we can sense God's intentions and become available to God's power. We can wield God's grace in situations where grace is needed. Let me give you an example of what I mean.

I experienced this awareness of God's presence and the wielding of grace in the writing and publication of my previous book, *Becoming a Blessed Church*. That was a book I had felt called to write for more than nine years, but I always sensed that the timing wasn't right. I had wanted to write a book that integrated the spiritual into the life of a congregation in a way that would call the whole community into a sense of prayerfulness and awareness of God's presence, yet in a way that was different from how spirituality has often been dealt with by the mainline church. I had noticed that many mainline congregations have tried to become spiritually aware by offering classes and retreats on spirituality. The problem, though, is that when spirituality is dealt with in that way, it is often treated as an add-on to the life of the church, not as something essential. Spirituality becomes another educational topic, along with every other educational topic, such as "history of the Bible," "the theology of Creation," and "when will Jesus return." I had a vision that the spiritual could become the life at the center of a church. I had wanted to write a book on bringing spirituality to the core of a church since before I began intensively studying spirituality as part of a doctoral program. Still, I realized that to do so, I had to develop a model that worked in a church, and so I came to my present church, Calvin Presbyterian Church, hoping to do so.

After about five years at Calvin, I sensed that I was ready to write the book, but I wasn't sure if God was ready for me to write it. So in 2000 I asked God in prayer whether it was time to write the book. I sensed God saying, "Not yet." After that, I approached God about three times a year in prayer, asking if it was time to write the book. Each time I sensed that the answer was "not yet." So I wrote other books on the spiritual life and how to live more integrated lives, books such as *Paradoxes for Living* and *Discovering the Narrow Path.*

Then in January 2003 I finally sensed that God was saying yes. It was a strange moment, because for the three previous years I had kept hearing in my heart, "Not yet." When I finally sensed God saying yes, it was like a Gideon moment (found in Judges 6:36–40, where Gideon keeps coming up with tests to be sure God's words are true). I wanted more assurance, and I was tempted to ask God to make the grass dewy and a sheepskin dry, and then vice versa. I resisted that temptation and started writing. Over the course of the next year I wrote, and throughout the writing actively sensed God's hand on my shoulder, and almost, at times, God's voice whispering in my ear. I wrote the book, having no idea who would publish it. I finished writing the book in late January 2004.

A week after finishing it, I received a telephone call in my office at the church. On the line was an editor, Beth Gaede, from the Alban Institute, an organization devoted to helping congregations become healthier. Beth had heard from someone else that I had some interesting ideas about another topic and wanted to know if I was interested in turning those ideas into a book. I told her that the ideas really merited only an article, not a whole book. Pausing, I figured that I might as well as tell her about the book I had just finished writing, titled *Becoming a Blessed Church.* I asked her if she was interested in hearing about it. She said yes, so I described the book.

Even as I described it, I was a bit reluctant because of what I knew about the books Alban had been publishing. The Alban

Institute had a great reputation, and many of its previous publications and seminars helped me in my ministry, but my experience was that Alban books tended to emphasize a more sociological, psychological, family-systems, and corporate-management approach to helping churches become healthier. I was reluctant to have the Institute publish my book, because it was spiritual in theme, even if it did integrate psychology, sociology, and corporate-management ideas. I wasn't sure that the book would sell with Alban's readers.

When I finished describing the book to Beth, I heard nothing but silence on the other end. After almost 10 seconds of silence, 10 seconds during which I was thinking, "See, they wouldn't know what to do with my book," she said, "Sorry for the silence. I just had chills go up my spine and I'm shaking a little bit. I just got out of a meeting with our director of publishing an hour ago. We had been talking about how we needed to change the direction of our books and move away from books on church growth and conflict management and into books on bringing spirituality into the church. We then outlined a particular book that we felt we needed to find someone to write. The problem is that we didn't know whom to ask. For the last 15 minutes you've been describing the very book that we had outlined. And you've already written it!"

My experience throughout the writing and eventual publication of the book was one of God's continual presence. I've experienced this same level of God's presence throughout my ministry and leadership. Again, developing an intuitive, integrative awareness of God's presence in all situations is crucial to forming a deep mystical intelligence in our leadership.

Ultimately, I believe that mystical intelligence is an integration of different kinds of awareness and intelligence. Mystical intelligence requires an integration of cognitive reason, emotional awareness, and something Adrian van Kaam calls "transconsiousness." What you'll notice is that mystical intelligence doesn't replace other forms of intelligence but enhances them by adding another dimension. Cognitive reason requires intellectual intelligence. Emotional awareness requires emotional intelligence. Mystical intelligence incorporates them, but adds a deeper awareness that is in tune with our transconsious, which integrates both our aspirations (yearning for God) and inspirations (the deeply sensed in-breathings of God into our mind, heart, and soul).[17]

The transconscious is a level of consciousness that goes beyond conscious or unconscious awareness. This level of consciousness is connected to the transcendent, to the inspirations of the Holy Spirit who speaks to us from the eternal. Just as we can live unaware of unconscious motivations and unresolved conflicts that cause certain behaviors in us, behaviors that counselors have to help us resolve, we can also live in ignorance of our transconscious. While the transconscious is a dimension of consciousness that is connected to the sacred and divine, it is also easy to ignore because it's a deep, rather than a surface, consciousness. Like the unconscious, it lies deep within our psyche, connecting it with God at levels that the conscious mind doesn't easily access.

Mystical intelligence arises out of the transconscious, so that we live in openness to the sacred and divine in everything. By becoming open transconsciously, we develop an intuitive, integrative awareness of God's presence in all situations that helps us to lead others in God's direction. When we are transconsciously aware, we sense God's presence and guidance at deep levels beyond normal perception. It's the depth of this awareness that causes others to be skeptical of our discernments. What we sense is not readily apparent to others, and sometimes it's only faintly apparent to us.

2. *An acceptance and expectation of providence.* Mystical intelligence is more than just a passive awareness of transconscious inspirations. It is an active embrace of God's providence acting in all situations. William Temple, the early 20th-century archbishop of Canterbury, is reported to have said, "I find that when I pray coincidences happen. When I cease to pray coincidences stop happening."[18] Temple is describing the experience of divine providence. When we have mystical intelligence, we discover providence working throughout our lives, and instead of labeling it mere coincidence, we embrace it as God's activity in our lives.

Rationally functional Christians and non-Christians are too quick to dismiss providence as pure coincidence without ever considering whether it could be the work of God's hand. There are always rational explanations as to why something couldn't be wrought by God's hand, and many Christians are quick to reject God's providence. For example, I remember once discussing God's providence and the sense of God's presence with a member of my family. We were driving in Canada, and we were discussing all sorts of religious matters. I had mentioned that I often experienced God's guidance and direction in my life, and sometimes I could sense what God was about to do.

My passenger immediately scoffed at me, saying that we simply could not see what God was about to do. He dismissed what I had said, as well as my whole approach to ministry and life by telling me that I was being ridiculous. I then did something that I rarely do. I decided to try to give him proof. I said, "Okay, I'll show you what I mean." At the time we were driving through a construction zone and were behind a large truck going 25 miles an hour in a 50-miles-an-hour zone (actually, it was all in kilometers, but I won't make you do the math). My traveling companion was getting very frustrated at the slow pace and was cursing the truck. I stopped and prayed for God to give me guidance on what to say; what I sensed was, "Tell him that this truck will turn off the road in 10 seconds." So that's what I told him. Literally 10 seconds later, the truck turned off the road. I said, "See, this is what I'm talking about." He then proceeded to tell me that I was ridiculous, that anyone could have seen that the truck was about to turn off, and that it wasn't evidence of God at all. I argued back, but eventually I silently prayed to God to give me more guidance, and what I sensed was God saying, "If he can't believe that, especially when it was apparent that the truck could have stayed on the road for much longer if it was carrying a load away, then he won't believe anything else." I dropped the matter.

Mystical intelligence recognizes, expects, and embraces providence in all situations. I identify with what William Temple said because I sense providence working so often in my life. I cannot imagine ministry without it. For example, I experienced this same providence surrounding my eventual doctoral studies in spirituality.

In 1989, a year after I had been ordained as an associate pastor in the first church I served, I was a frustrated pastor. I had high hopes for ministry, but I was struggling. I wanted to be a catalyst to help people experience God and God's presence, but I was stuck in a cerebral church in which God was more of a thought that an experience. I was also part of the Presbyterian denomination, and the truth is that a big problem among us Presbyterians is that our faith is generally centered too much in our heads. We treat God as an abstract thought or problem to be figured out. I was tired of being in that kind of church, in that kind of denomination, and of being that kind of pastor. My problem wasn't with the members of the church itself but with the intellectualistic tradition we followed. I wanted to learn how to lead people to something more, something deeper, something more spiritual, but I didn't know how.

I had heard of a program in spirituality at Duquesne University, in Pittsburgh, Pennsylvania—a program that had attracted me for several years. Still, I wasn't ready to go back to school. I figured that maybe when I was 40 I could go back to school and study spirituality. At the same time, I was spiritually hungry and wanted to help people who were spiritually hungry. But I kept all of these thoughts and feelings crammed in the back of my mind for a future date.

One day I was invited to a wedding, and I really had no idea why. I knew the bride only vaguely. I knew her mother a bit better, but not much. The mother of the bride was involved at the time in leading pilgrimages to Medjugorje, in what used to be Yugoslavia. You may have heard of Medjugorje. During the 1980s, several teens reported seeing apparitions of the Virgin Mary. Many people flocked there to see the Virgin, and many had healing experiences. I think I was invited to the wedding because I had an interest in healing prayer, and therefore in Medjugorje, which the mother of the bride knew.

I think she may have had another motive, a motive she wasn't all that aware of: to be a conduit of divine providence. At the reception, the mother pulled me aside and said, "Graham, I have to introduce you to Father Rick Byrne. He is the priest who celebrated the wedding mass. He's also the executive director of the spirituality program at Duquesne. You have a lot in common. You should talk." With that she left Rick and me alone. Rick and I sat down for a long time and talked about spirituality. It was a great conversation. Afterward, we agreed that we should meet again and talk about my going to Duquesne to get my Ph.D. in spirituality. We exchanged cards, promising to call each other. Neither of us did.

Months went by, and I kept thinking about the program, but I couldn't figure out how to find the time to do it. Then, a month later, I was at the health club where I was a member. I had just finished playing racquetball, and as I was changing in the locker room I looked at the guy next to me. It was Rick Byrne. I had never seen him there before. Both of us realized that this coincidence might be the Spirit trying to get us together for me to go to Duquesne. This time we did make an appointment. I ended up going to Duquesne and getting my Ph.D. It changed my whole life and ministry. From it I learned a whole different way of being a pastor and "doing church," a way that grounded what I did in prayer and seeking God's will.

This is the way providence works, and those with mystical intelligence not only accept it but expect and embrace it. It is almost as though they have a radar that always scans the horizon for providential acts and circumstances. And because they do, they experience God's hand in everything.

3. *A passionate desire to make God's will a priority.* It's not enough to have an intuitive, integrative awareness of God's presence, or to embrace and expect providence. Before we can develop this awareness and expectation, we must first have a passionate desire to make God's will a priority. This may seem obvious, but I've found through my own experiences that while many, many Christians, especially Christian leaders, talk the talk of putting God's will first, very few seek God's will with a passion in the minutiae of life. When it comes down to seeking God's will in their conversations with others, making small decisions (and even large ones), and determining what course to take, they resort to rationally or emotionally based decision-making processes.

Unfortunately, most of us are so accustomed to acting in a functional way, a way rooted in making decisions based on our own criteria, that we fail to seek God's will and ways in the large and small events of life. Those who have a passionate desire to make God's will a priority have an accompanying intolerance of functionalism. As I mentioned earlier, functionalism is the tendency to reduce matters to a rational, logical perspective, focusing on the pragmatic rather than the possible. It discounts spiritual discernment by emphasizing human analysis, operations, and performance. When we lead from the functional, we root decisions and actions in human perspectives rather than try to open ourselves to God's perspectives.

I don't want to give the impression that having mystical intelligence means being unaware or unconcerned about functional matters. Budgets, plans, and practical tasks and strategies are important. We need to make plans. We need to set budgets. We need to create organization and order. We need to deal with the practical matters of our families, work, and personal lives. When we integrate mystical intelligence, we also use other forms of intelligence. In the process, we put the functional under the guidance of the spiritual. We ask first what God is calling us to do, and as we sense the answer, then we go about doing the functional things that bring God's will to fruition.

Seeking God's will—having a longing for God's will—isn't a factor just in making board decisions. It has to do with how we treat others in times of conflict, how we resolve family disputes, and how we determine what jobs we will take. Those with mystical intelligence seek God's will in small and large events. They have a passion for wanting to do God's will everywhere in their lives. There's a connection between this passion and God's activity, for the more we have a longing to seek and do God's will, the more we find God's hand in everything we do. The missionary mystic Frank Laubach wrote about this experience of God's presence in everything. Laubach turned his life into an experiment of prayer in which he sought God's will and way in everything, attempting to become deeply open to God in every moment. Doing this, he discovered amazing things happening in his life as a result. He wrote about his experiences:

I feel simply carried along each hour, doing my part in a plan which is far beyond myself. This sense of cooperation with God in little things is what so astonishes me, for I never have felt this way before. I need something, and turn around to find it waiting for me. I must work, to be sure, but there is God working along with me. God takes care of all the rest. My part is to live this hour in continuous inner conversation with God and in perfect responsiveness to his will, to make this hour gloriously rich.[19]

When we have mystical intelligence, we develop a drive to put God's concerns first, even if these concerns seem impractical or require a change in perspective. In fact, mystical intelligence often requires a change in perspective, because as we look at the world through mystical perceptions, we find that we have to engage in actions and activities that change and transform us. Henry Blackaby and Claude King, Southern Baptist writers who are adept at culling the mystical dimension of the evangelical tradition, discuss these changes in their book *Experiencing God*. They present seven realities of experiencing God, saying that as we give ourselves to God in faith, the Spirit leads us through certain experiences that challenge and transform us.[20] For example, we realize that God is always working around us, always pursues with us a loving relationship that is real and personal, continually invites us to become partners in God's work, and in the midst of all this, speaks through everything and every event to reveal God's self, purposes, and ways.

Blackaby and King also point out two disturbing realities, especially for those who expect tangible rewards for their faith. They point out that as we join God in an ever-deepening relationship, two things consistently happen. First, joining God in God's work *leads us to a crisis of belief that requires faith and action.*[21] Most of us are under the assumption that the more we act in faith, the easier things should get. King and Blackaby say that the opposite generally happens. Things don't get easier. Instead we end up coming to a point where we aren't sure what to do. There's little clarity. We are faced with decisions that might lead to something positive or negative, and we have no guarantees. We have no choice but to act on faith. We have to trust in God and trust in our discernment of God's will. This is where leadership and mystical intelligence intersect, because we have to have confidence in a course of action that has no proof of success. Often we face a crisis in which we have to decide between the functional way that offers us more control and certainty and our discernment of God's will, a way that is a way rife with uncertainty.

For example, in following the functional way we might ask, "Do we have the money to do this?" The way of faith and action asks, "Are we called to this, and if we are, can we trust that the money will be there in the end?" Certainly taking the second path leads to a sense of crisis, even if it's a minor one, because we aren't sure of the outcome. Leading people along the path of faith and discernment is hard as a leader, because people who forcefully advocate a more functional path surround us and are glad to lead people in a more comfortable, functional direction.

If we survive this small crisis, we face another reality. Blackaby and King tell us that we must *make major adjustments in our lives to join God in what God is doing.*[22] This necessity takes us a step further into determining whether we have a passion for Christ's will; for joining God in God's work means being willing to be changed and transformed. We have to change how we think, how we see, and how we react to the world. Or more precisely, we have to become open to God's transforming work in our lives. Being open to God's transformation takes us back to chapter 1, where we discussed the nature of humble leadership—leadership that is radically open to God and that chooses God's path over one that appears more certain, but that in reality closes us to God's path.

Allowing ourselves to be transformed is the fundamental task faced by every humble leader, especially those with mystical intelligence. It is also the basic task of every congregation. Few leaders, members, or churches want to be transformed. They want to remain the same. My contention is that most Christians are OK with God so long as God changes the world. It's when God changes us instead of the world that we balk. This is the test of how strong our passion is for God's will. When it is strong, we are willing to say to God, "You are the potter, I am the clay." Mystical intelligence has an aptitude for understanding the necessity and processes of transformation—of having to make major adjustments in our lives and congregations to join God in what God is doing.

As humble leaders, we use our mystical intelligence not only to gain a sense of what God is doing and leading us to do, but also to discern and determine how God is calling us to change ourselves so that we can become transformed. As Paul says in Romans, "Do not be conformed to this world, but be transformed by the renewing of your minds, so that you may discern what is the will of God—what is good and acceptable and perfect" (Rom. 12:2).

In the end, mystical intelligence contributes to Spirit-led leadership by opening us at intuitive, integrative levels to an awareness of God's presence in all situations; by giving us an acceptance and expectation of providence; and by emerging out of and nurturing an ever-deepening desire to make God's will a priority. Mystical intelligence gives us an intellectual framework in which we can look at life from a more spiritual perspective that allows us to see spiritual potential in every area of life.

Mystical intelligence becomes the mental component of a whole way of leadership that is grounded in leading people out of self-determined directions and in God's direction, a direction discerned by the community of leaders, refined, and then acted upon. It is a difficult way of leadership because it requires a high level of skill and confidence—the skill to lead people in uncertain directions and the confidence to keep going even in the midst of doubters and skeptics. It is always much easier to follow a more functional path. In fact, it is much easer to take either the reactive or the proactive path over the Spirit-active path because both of those paths remain under human control. There is a way of leadership that potentially has more power and more lasting influence—if we are willing to have the faith and perseverance to adopt that way.

6

Humbly Effective Leadership

+ ⊫◆⊐ +

Then Jesus called the twelve together and gave them power and au-
thority over all demons and to cure diseases, and he sent them out to
proclaim the kingdom of God and to heal. He said to them, "Take noth-
ing for your journey, no staff, nor bag, nor bread, nor money—not
even an extra tunic. Whatever house you enter, stay there, and leave
from there. Wherever they do not welcome you, as you are leaving
that town shake the dust off your feet as a testimony against them."
They departed and went through the villages, bringing the good news
and curing diseases everywhere.

Luke 9:1–6

NOW THAT YOU'VE REACHED THIS POINT IN THE BOOK, YOU MAY HAVE
noticed a problem that afflicts most books on leadership, including this one. The problem is that leadership books are heavy on
theory but light on the connection between theory and practice.
If any field of study is plagued by the struggle to connect theory
with practice it is that of leadership, especially spiritual leadership. Why? Because a thorough understanding of leadership is
elusive. It is almost impossible to quantify or even qualify what
makes a good leader. It's like asking what makes a great baseball
pitcher. Of the many great pitchers, few share common traits.
Some are great fastballers. Some are great knuckleballers. The
traits are different, but the greatness is the common denomina-
tor. Good leaders have some traits in common, but not all share
the same traits.

We seem to recognize good leaders inherently when we are
in their presence, yet they are not built the same. Some are intro-
verts. Others are extroverts. Some speak a lot, outlining in detail

their visions and strategies. Others are reticent, communicating vision and strategy with an economy of words. Some are bundles of energy, dipping a finger into everything, while others are better at energizing those around them to work independently. There is no single right way to be a great leader, much to the consternation of those who seek that "one right way" to lead.

Consequently, writers on leadership stay on safe ground by remaining in the theoretical arena. The danger of getting too practical is that we won't cover all possible scenarios, or we will end up endorsing a personal style of leadership that people with different personalities cannot embrace. For example, if we teach that leaders should listen more and act less, we could unintentionally stifle leaders by making them hesitant to give direction when it would be appropriate to do so. In addition, we could end up trying to turn an extroverted leader into an introverted one, thereby diminishing those very skills that may make the person an effective leader. It is difficult to be simultaneously theoretical and practical. For this reason, most leadership writers stay theoretical. It allows them to focus more on principles of leadership in a context where it is recognized that there is no *one* right way to be a leader. Still, humble leaders do seem to share similar foundations, such as the foundational principles advocated in this book: being self-aware, prayerful, unifying, and Spirit-led.

While building a strong theoretical foundation is crucial, humble leaders must also develop a certain set of *skills* to be effective. The failure to develop these basic skills accounts for why most people would never think to connect humility with leadership. Most people think a humble leader would be hesitant to give strong direction, take charge of a situation, and enforce discipline when necessary, and as a result they would be ineffective. Despite their misconceptions, many truly great leaders are humble *and* effective. As I mentioned in chapter 1, Jim Collins, a business researcher, found a strong connection between great leadership and humility, and great leaders in the corporate world tend to be both humble and effective.[1]

The great example he gives is of Darwin Smith, who in 1971 became CEO of Kimberly-Clark, a paper company with declining sales. Many thought that he was the wrong choice at the time because, as a mild-mannered, in-house attorney, he didn't seem to have the qualifications to enable the company to grow. But apparently he did. Over his 20-year tenure, he turned Kimberly-Clark into the leading paper company in the world. Collins says:

> A man who carried no airs of self-importance, Smith found his favorite companionship among plumbers and electricians and spent his vacations rumbling around his Wisconsin farm in the cab of a backhoe, digging holes and moving rocks. He never cultivated hero status or executive celebrity status. When a journalist asked him to describe his management style, Smith, dressed unfashionably like a farm boy wearing his first suit bought at J.C. Penny, just stared back from the other side of his nerdy-looking black-rimmed glasses. After a long, uncomfortable silence, he said simply: "Eccentric . . ."
>
> But if you were to think of Darwin Smith as somehow meek or soft, you would be terribly mistaken. His awkward shyness and lack of pretense was coupled with a fierce, even stoic, resolve toward life.[2]

Obviously Smith was not a congregational leader, but leadership is leadership, whether in the church or in the corporate world. He exemplified how leaders can be both humble and effective. The qualities that made him humble weren't the clothes he wore or the people he associated with. Instead, what made him humble was the sense he had that he wasn't all-important. He was serving a company, and the company was what mattered. For the humble congregational leader, humility comes in our willingness simply to serve God in guiding our churches to follow God's direction.

Being a humble leader requires a merging of a humble spiritual disposition and approach to life with a certain set of skills that allow us to be effective as leaders. These are skills that work in consonance with a humble presence, allowing us to become open to God's presence and guidance while simultaneously finding a way to move others in God's direction. Five skills enable the leader to be effective while maintaining a humble foundation.

SURROUND OURSELVES WITH GOOD LEADERS
AND LET THEM SHINE

To be an effective, humble leader it is crucial to surround ourselves with other effective, humble leaders. This wisdom may seem to be a given, but my experience in both the churches I've served and those I've consulted with is that this step is too often ignored. It is generally easier for churches to settle for poor, ego-driven leaders (or sometimes those with no leadership ability at all) rather than good, humble ones because accepting them is the path of least resistance. The problem churches face is that they need to fill a leadership position, and instead of doing the work to uncover and nurture a good, humble leader, they choose a person who either has already been leading or who is already involved and is willing to say yes to becoming a leader. This is especially true in smaller churches where the pool of high-quality leaders may be small.

In the end, much of the success or failure of a ministry comes down to whether a person can lead. This may seem a bit like a conundrum or a paradox, but the best leaders recruit the best leaders. They inherently understand that it is difficult or impossible to turn someone lacking in leadership skills into a confident and competent leader. So they focus on recruiting those who already have good leadership skills, or those who have the potential, with a little training, to develop these skills. It is important not to settle for poor leaders but instead to seek them out and then do everything possible to help them shine in their ministries. We have to give them every opportunity, whether it is reducing the sting of their failures, helping them clarify and simplify their ministry, or giving them responsibility for their own success or failure.

While it is important to recruit those with strong leadership skills or the potential to build them, it is essential to recruit humble people into leadership. While we have our antennae attuned to finding already skillful leaders, we need to put much more emphasis on assessing their openness to God, their willingness to serve, and their readiness to let go of their own pride. I always figure that it is easier to teach an inexperienced yet humble person with potential how to lead, than it is to teach a prideful, ego-driven, yet experienced, leader to become humble. In fact, I believe so strongly in the need to recruit humble leaders that I would suggest that if you have only a small pool of humble leaders, it is better to shrink the ministry of the church so that it can be led by humble leaders than to have a much larger ministry led by more prideful leaders. (Of course, this is not a hard-and-fast rule.)

Ever since I became a pastor, I've been fascinated with the methods used in most mainline churches to recruit lay leaders. What I've found almost across the board is that struggling churches generally recruit lay leaders whose main strength lies in one of three areas: they have been good workers in the church over time, they have been managers of some sort in their jobs, or they are wealthy and financially influential. These attributes aren't necessarily harmful in lay leaders, but they can create conditions in which we end up calling forth people who either aren't leaders, aren't humble, or are neither.

For instance, many good and faithful church workers are considered "good and faithful" precisely because they are reliable. They are good followers, but they aren't necessarily great at leading others. They often lack the ability to conceive and delegate a task or project, skills we will discuss later. Often they end up frustrated because they want others to help, but they don't know how to ask for help. Their anger builds because others haven't picked up the slack, yet the irony is that these leaders haven't left any slack for others to pick up. We may have given these individuals a leadership *role*, even though they lack the skills. The result is frustration on everyone's part.

In a previous church I served, one leader was a fantastic church worker, but when he led a committee, he ran it into the ground. So long as the task was simple and could be done by him alone, he was fine. But if the assignment was a complicated one that required planning and parceling out jobs, he became frantic and frustrated. During one event that he coordinated, he did everything, and everyone marveled at his imagination and stamina. Afterward, he blasted his committee for failing to help

him more. The committee members were stunned. They had just
finished praising him, exclaiming that they had never seen such
a competent, thorough person. They couldn't understand why
he was so angry. What *they* didn't understand was that in his
mind, they hadn't supported him because they didn't help. What
he didn't understand was that he had left them with no specific
tasks to help with. He had already done everything to the last
detail. He was clearly a good worker but a poor leader because
he couldn't delegate. In the end, being forced into the leadership role caused him to become narcissistic and self-pitying. The
whole project became about him: what he had to do and how
people failed to help him.

Many other church leaders are chosen primarily because of
their experience leading in the secular sphere. It is assumed that
if they are good at leading in the "real" world, they must be good
at leading in the church. Unfortunately, this is not always the
case. Sometimes the ability to lead in a secular arena is a disad-
vantage in a church, especially if we are seeking humble leaders.
In the best secular organizations, leadership is humble, collegial,
and collaborative. Regrettably, there are too few *exceptional* organizations. Too many mediocre managers and leaders emphasize
expediency and efficiency over creativity and quality. At the office, they may lead by intimidation, mind games, imperial commands, or manipulation. Many of these leaders are also church
members. The fact that a person leads in her job doesn't mean
that she is good at it.

Again, let me offer an example. In my first church I once visited a sick parishioner, a young woman in her early 30s. During my visit she complained about one of our church's leaders,
saying that seeing him serve communion as an elder in worship
made her feel queasy. Why? Because she had had business deal-
ings with him on a regular basis, and recently, when her sup-
plier ran out of a product and she couldn't deliver on time, he
screamed at her in a profanity-laced tirade, threatening to destroy her reputation and career. Should this kind of person be a
leader in the church? Ironically, the leadership style that was at
least somewhat effective for him at work made him ineffectual at
the church. He wasn't free to lead in the brash, intimidating way

he was accustomed to in the workplace, so he really ended up doing nothing because he hadn't developed other skills.

Finally, some leaders are chosen simply because they are wealthy and financially influential. Again, this does not lead to humble leadership. Too many wealthy leaders use their wealth to manipulate churches, especially ones with poorer members. What does it say when leaders are chosen primarily because of their financial clout or ability to intimidate?

Humble leaders have to be discerned, rather than chosen. In my book *Becoming a Blessed Church,* I offer a process for choosing leaders through prayer and discernment. Ideally, the best way to find humble leaders is to let God lead us to them. At the center of this process are several basic questions we can ask about potential leaders: "Is this person humble and prayerful, and does she have leadership qualities? Is this person more interested in his own agenda or in seeking God's agenda? Will this person lead others to prayerful discernment?" Just asking these question changes the dynamic of the search for leaders. It puts the onus on recruiting humble and prayerful people, rather than on their functional abilities and skills. Again, it is much easier to teach a person how to lead than it is to teach her how to become humble.

Once we have these leaders in place, it is important to let them do what they do, which is lead. Too often pastoral leaders are tempted to micromanage lay leaders, and lay leaders to micromanage other lay leaders, but it is difficult to create a healthy, growing congregation with micromanagers in charge. We need to let humble leaders do what they do and to help them develop confidence by enabling them to succeed in what they do. We will talk more about how to enable them to succeed in the next few sections.

ELICIT IDEAS, SEEK GOD'S GUIDANCE, AND SET A DIRECTION

During the 1980s many people became fans of the television show *Star Trek: The Next Generation.* The show succeeded despite the skeptics who doubted that it could ever become anywhere near as good as the original *Star Trek* television show. The creators and writers of *The Next Generation* were very creative in making it distinct from the original. One of the best decisions was to create a captain who was dramatically different from the original one, a leader unlike those normally seen on television or in movies. The typical leader in a TV drama or movie is strong, independent, and decisive, someone who quickly and resolutely dispenses orders and solves problems. This new *Star Trek* leader, Captain Jean-Luc Picard, was unlike those typical leaders, including his predecessor on the original show, Captain James T. Kirk.

What made Picard so different? Picard modeled a uniquely democratic style of leadership that encouraged other leaders to be fully part of the process. He elicited ideas, determined the best one, and set a direction. His style of leadership was distinct enough that it spawned a leadership book, *Make It So: Leadership Lessons from* Star Trek: The Next Generation.[3]

For us fans of *Star Trek*, watching Jean-Luc Picard each week was something of a revelation. His style was suited both to responding to imminent danger and to thinking through perplexing problems or situations. In a crisis, Picard would quickly elicit ideas by shouting out to the other officers, "Options!" They, in turn, would offer quick and succinct suggestions. Sometimes Picard would go with their ideas. At other times he would integrate several ideas into a better plan. When given more time, he would withdraw with his senior leaders into a conference room, asking for suggestions, allowing for discussion and dialogue, and then integrating all of them into a more comprehensive plan. His remarkable ability both elicited maximum participation from other leaders and created maximum cohesion.

I do realize (to assure those of you who aren't fans) that this was a television show rather than reality, but it modeled for many of us a humble *and* effective leadership style. Too often leaders (including pastors and laity) let their ego and pride control them. They worry too much about failure, not being given enough credit for success, or being subverted. In the process, they never let their ministries rise above mediocrity. Even though they may serve on boards, committees, and task forces, they are uncomfortable leading a process that allows for both full participation and decisiveness. Often they gravitate toward one or the other. Either they allow for full participation as a way of masking their fear of making a decision while secretly avoiding making decisions, or they are overcontrolling, locking others out of the process.

How do we lead others in a process that allows for full participation and decisiveness? First, we need to recognize that the Holy Spirit speaks through different voices and that the Spirit may be speaking through many people in the decision-making process. The more we respect the fact that the Spirit can speak through even the least of the voices around us, the more we discover creativity in those voices. I've become so enamored with the idea that the Spirit can speak through any voice that I'm sometimes guilty of slowing the decision-making process too much in my attempt to elicit full participation. If I sense that other perspectives haven't been heard, I will suggest that we take a month to pray over a matter before deciding. Sometimes we don't need that month. But I'd rather be guilty of unnecessarily slowing a process than of ignoring the potential voice of the Spirit.

Another way we invite full participation is by reducing competitiveness, constantly reminding members that we are all in a process of discerning God's will, not our own. It's very easy for people on a board, committee, or task force to seek mainly what they want and to compete for power. One way I decrease competitiveness is by saying something along the lines of, "Remember as you advocate for your idea that the focus is on trying to figure out what God wants. Your voice is part of that, but so are the others'. Share your ideas, but don't become so wedded to them that you forget what our real purpose is: seeking what God wants." In keeping with this tactic, I always try to encourage all members to participate, even if their ideas seem silly or irrelevant. I may disagree with them, but I try my best to be respectful. Ultimately, I always encourage people to seek God's solution, which is discerned together. The one danger with this approach is that people can use it to avoid making a decision as they engage in endless discussion. There is a balance to be kept in which we allow for fruitful dialogue but also make the decisions.

I also try to elicit full participation by taking time out to regroup and refocus whenever people become irritated or confrontational. I always work to keep our collective egos in check, including mine, so that what matters is not our desires but our communal ability to seek what God is willing us to do.

When we engage in this process, it is important to have the humility to recognize when a particular decision isn't working and the willingness to revisit it. Again, it does no good to embark on a course if the course doesn't work. In my 10-plus years as pastor of Calvin Church, we have changed course many times. We have tried many educational programs, many worship styles, and many schedules. We are always willing to jettison a decision if it doesn't seem to work, even after we've discerned that God wants us to do it. My assumption is not that God was wrong but that we didn't discern well enough—or that we did, but the timing wasn't right. One other possibility is that we are led down a difficult path that is meant to transform us. There are times when we do the best we can to come up with creative solutions and discern God's will and still discover that what we've decided isn't right or isn't right *yet*. The key is having the collective humility and adaptability always to seek God's new way, even if it means going back on what we earlier discerned to be God's will.

GIVE GUIDANCE AND LET GO

How often do you say the "Serenity Prayer," either in your heart or aloud? Millions of people worldwide, especially those recovering from addictions, have found comfort and wisdom in this famous prayer. The great 20th-century theologian Reinhold Niebuhr crafted it from other well-known prayers of the late 19th century. Christians have cherished it for years, and it is the central prayer for Alcoholics Anonymous. The best-known part of the prayer is as follows:

> God grant me the serenity to accept the things I cannot change;
> courage to change the things I can; and wisdom to know the
> difference.

It is hard to think of any prayer that gives better guidance for those seeking to be effective and humble leaders. At the center of the prayer is the wisdom to know when to *do* something, and when to *let it go* (or as it is said in the Twelve Steps, "Let go and let God"). There is a similar balance to be kept in leadership: knowing when to take on a task ourselves and when to delegate it. One of the biggest threats to forming a healthy, humble ministry is the failure of pastors and other leaders to delegate ministry to others.

Delegation of leadership and ministry is a delicate balancing act because we have both to relinquish control and to hold people accountable. If we delegate too much without asking people to be accountable, there's always the threat that the ministries they are leading will crumble. I've seen that several times in my ministry. I've delegated ministries to others, only to see them fail to follow through with simple tasks, stop holding meetings, or flounder because they tried to do everything themselves while failing to delegate tasks to others.

When leaders don't delegate *and* hold people accountable, it becomes difficult for pastoral and lay leadership to do ministry. The temptation is either to reclaim the ministry and do it ourselves, or to ignore the failures in our fear of offending others. The problem is that refusing to delegate can lead us either to burnout because we are doing too much, or to frustration because others aren't doing enough. So how do we delegate *and* hold people accountable? I tend to hold several principles of delegation.

The first principle is a lesson I learned from a sixth-century monk and mystic named Dorotheos of Gaza, whom I mentioned in chapter 1. The lesson is that in the face of another's failure to take up a ministry, we *accuse ourselves rather than others*. Dorotheos was the epitome of humility. Early on in his life, he was often criticized and made the butt of practical jokes by others in his monastic community, but as time passed he became an icon of wisdom for his fellow monks. He lived a harsh life in the desert as a member of a monastic community. Theirs was not a plush monastery by any means. Each monk lived in a small hut among venomous scorpions, snakes, and stinging insects. They had little food and devoted their days to prayer. Dorotheos taught that the humble way is always the best way, and the key to humility is always to accuse ourselves when we are at odds with another.[4]

His guidance was that even if we find that the other person is at fault, we should strive to discover within ourselves how we might have contributed to that fault.

How does self-accusation relate to leadership, considering that I just said that we need to hold others accountable? When delegating, it is easy to see how others have failed to do what they said they would. We may hold the other person accountable, but we fail to join them by simultaneously holding ourselves accountable. I've found that even though it is easy to detect others' faults, I can work to detect how I failed to give enough instruction or guidance. By sharing the blame for failure, I not only hold the other person accountable, but I become accountable for helping resolve the problem.

One of the biggest mistakes we make as leaders in a congregation is assuming that because we have certain insights, abilities, and skills, others must also have them. This is not always the case. I've realized over the years that the more educated we get, and the more skills we develop, the more we forget what it was like to do the same things before receiving that training. For instance, before going to seminary and receiving education and training as a therapist and spiritual director, how did I see the church and its operations? Truthfully, I don't remember. What I do know is that I have insights into organization and management that many church leaders don't. When I make the assumption that they understand what I understand, I make a big mistake. They may understand, but to make that assumption is a fault. The first step in holding others accountable is holding ourselves simultaneously accountable.

One way I hold myself accountable when others fail or do not follow through is to ask what I can do to make their job easier. It's not often hard to find what I could have done. I don't want to sound as though I never slip and blame others, but I do *try* to lead by recognizing my own faults first. If I can, I take responsibility for the failure and then try to help the other find a better way to complete the task or activity.

A second principle of delegation: I do my best to make sure that whatever the leadership tasks are, they *are relatively clear*—at least insofar as possible. With some leadership tasks, it is difficult to be clear, especially with ministries that are complicated or for which there is no precedent. What often causes laity to fail in their leadership tasks is their inexperience in church ministry and unfamiliarity with the way things work in a church. For instance, in a church in which there is no identified Christian education director, often education ministries are left under the direction of a church member who may or may not be trained in education. He can easily get overwhelmed with choosing curriculum, recruiting teachers, and creating new educational programs. The leader may need help understanding what tasks or activities are a priority. He may need help in determining what the mission of the ministry is. He may need help in clarifying his ministry's mandate.

Often confusion begins with a leader's not knowing what the ministry she is leading is supposed to do. We assume that a leader naturally comprehends the scope of the ministry, only to find out later that the leader did not. I believe this is a huge problem in the mainline church: the fact that ministries have been passed down for years without our reviewing their purpose and responsibility. Our churches generally are fairly old—50, 100, 150, or even 200-plus years, although the problem of new leaders not understanding their mandate can exist even in newer churches. Ministry has been passed down not only from leader to leader but also from generation to generation. We may assume that the mandate of a committee is clear because it's been running for years, but this isn't always the case. We may have to spend time with newer leaders to make sure that they understand what they are leading and how to do it. This guidance is valid for pastors guiding lay leaders and for lay leaders guiding other lay leaders.

Also, in the process of helping a leader gain clarity, we can at times help them simplify their ministry by breaking down their tasks into smaller steps. I learned how important simplification of steps is from running a behavior-modification program with adolescents and children in a psychiatric hospital. Behavior modification is a system of creating "reinforcers" that either modify good behaviors or extinguish problematic behaviors. In running the program, we found that one of the biggest reasons we failed to modify a problem behavior was that we were asking the kids to take too sophisticated a step. Often the troubled adolescents and children didn't know how to behave better. They needed clearer instructions on what constituted good behavior. For instance, one boy we worked with reacted to limit-setting in angry, violent ways. He was quick to spin out of control by hitting, spitting, and biting anyone who tried to discipline him or say no. He would get so out of control that we would have to put him a time-out room—a room with no furniture and a small observation window in the door where violent children could stay until they had observably calmed down. Sometimes it would take four adult staff members to restrain the child as he squirmed, spit, bit, dug fingernails into our arms, and kicked us.

One new insight about him was that even though reacting nonviolently was simple for us, he had been controlling his family for years through his violent outbursts. They always capitulated when he threatened violence, and if they didn't he escalated his violent outbursts until they did. When he came into the hospital, he had never been around adults who didn't kowtow to him. So his response in face of the limits we set was to escalate his violent behavior exponentially. We quickly ran into a problem. We were disciplining him so much and putting him into the time-out room so often that he wasn't getting better. Everything was too negative. The problem: he simply didn't know how to react in a nonviolent way. He couldn't see an alternative. So we had to figure out how to simplify the steps towards nonviolence. In the end, we set up a system in which even in the midst of a violent outburst he could receive points (points were awarded for good behavior and could be used to obtain privileges) for expressing his feelings appropriately. And we simplified the process of learning new behavior for him by instructing him exactly how to express these feelings. If he used "I" statements such as, "I'm feeling angry. I'm upset at the way this person treated me. When you talk to me that way, it makes me feel happy," he could earn points. We always worked to simplify the process for him, and slowly he found healthier ways to deal with his anger and to accept limits.

The same principle of behavior modification, the principle of simplifying and clarifying the steps, applies to leadership. Often failures of leadership are a matter of leaders not knowing how to

carry out a task and not knowing how to ask for help in simplifying and clarifying the process. In addition, we don't necessarily do a good enough job of rewarding and reinforcing leaders
for what they do well, especially if they are simple accomplish-
ments. We can help leaders simply by helping them understand
what is essential and what isn't and also by praising them for the
simple tasks they do well. With all this advice in mind, I am not
advocating that we should be condescending. The point is never
to assume that lay leaders automatically know how to lead the
ministries we are asking them to lead. At the same time, we also
need to remember that they are mature, adult leaders and have
been chosen for their faith and skill. We simultaneously have to
let them bear responsibility for their leadership.

A third principle is *to let people fail.* This may seem to go
against what I've just said above about sharing the accountability, but the reality is that we reach a point at which we simply
have to give the leaders responsibility for succeeding or failing.
We have to let go of the ministries and let the other leaders become responsible for them. Relinquishing the responsibility can
be frustrating in a church because we want so much for every
ministry to succeed, yet the reality is that sometimes leaders fail,
and their ministries fail. Sometimes the leaders who have been
called forth simply aren't good at leading others. I estimate that
over the course of my ministry, about 35 percent of the things
we have tried to do have failed for one reason or another—poor
leadership (including poor leadership on my part), the fact that
God really didn't want to us to do that ministry, or that it was
not yet time. One way or another, propping up a failing ministry
does no one any good. At times in my ministry I have simply let
a poor leader fail, usually after I have tried to clarify and simplify
with little tangible result. At these times I just don't do anything.
I let them fail.

In the end, I've found that if I approach most situations with
a willingness to accept responsibility for my failures first, helping
others gain clarity about what they are doing, and then letting
others succeed or fail, the congregation and its leaders become
healthier.

Underlying these three principles is a much larger one: that
as leaders, our fundamental role is to be spiritual guides who

do our best to open people up to God's divine and often hidden hand, while simultaneously giving them the grace to be imperfect in their leadership. We are called to be humble and spiritual leaders to humble and spiritual leaders-in-training. We can't assume that because others are in leadership positions, they inherently know how to lead. We have to give them on-the-job training, which means lightening the load by sharing the blame when necessary, helping them gain clarity on how to lead, and then letting them walk or fall on their own.

ACCEPT CRITICISM, RESIST OFFENSE, AND PROVIDE SUPPORT

Ever since I became a pastor, I've lived with a fear, one that I think is shared by many pastors. It's the fear of "the phone call"—that call out of nowhere from a member of the church, ripping us apart for something we either did or didn't do. I feared "the call" much more during my first few years as a solo pastor, yet every once in a while when the phone rings in my office I feel apprehensive.

I'm not sure exactly what sparked my fear, but I've found it to be well grounded. I've received "the call" on numerous occasions. For instance, I received it two years into my ministry at Calvin Church from a woman who was furious because she hadn't been to church in six weeks and no one had called her. I tried to explain to her that most of the folk in the congregation knew that she was working on a master's degree and that she was working every other Sunday, so we didn't want to put pressure on her. I explained that we were trying to respect her privacy, which was true—but she was having none of it.

On another occasion, I received "the call" from someone who accused me of secretly wanting to get rid of the church's drama ministry. She told me that from the moment I had come to Calvin Church, I had wanted to get rid of it, and that my attitude showed this intention. It really didn't matter what I said. I was considered to be guilty as charged. The most I could say in my defense, which turned out to be a fairly powerful defense, was that the year before when the drama ministry was struggling financially to pay the rights fees for a play, an anonymous donor had donated the $600 to help the ministry buy the rights to the play—and that this anonymous donor was me. My defense seemed to work, even though the person came back a year later and accused me once again of wanting to get rid of the ministry. In fact, that ministry was one of the things that attracted me to Calvin Church. I suspect that the real problem was that on several occasions I did not side with the drama ministry when conflict between it and others arose. In the past, the drama ministry had always won these conflicts.

I've had many of these phone calls since I've been at Calvin Church, although they've diminished over the years. Of course, the method of communication has also changed in recent years. In modern life, "the phone call" has been replaced by "the e-mail." My fear of "the phone call" or "the e-mail" reveals a fact of ministry, and especially of leadership in a congregation: no matter how hard we try to lead a congregation to health, we will be criticized. We can't escape it. And sometimes that criticism will be unreasonably harsh. That's unavoidable, too.

What we can easily forget about churches, especially when we think about them in idealistic rather than pragmatic ways, is that they are filled with imperfect people. If you want a perfect church, you have to get rid of all the people, but if you get rid of all the people, you no longer have a church. The sooner we accept that churches are imperfect and that among the healthy members are some very troubled people, the sooner we are ready to engage in real ministry. And real ministry brings us face to face with people who struggle with basic rudeness, personality disorders, mental illness, and general brokenness. Fortunately, these people tend to be the exception rather than the rule in most congregations, but even these exceptions can make our lives miserable.

So how do we deal not only with "the phone call" but also with "the visit" or "the behind-our-backs accusation"? The first step is remembering the lesson of the coyote and the scorpion.

One day a scorpion approached a coyote and asked it if it would ferry the scorpion across the river. The coyote said, "No

way! If I put you on my back you'll sting me." The scorpion responded, "I wouldn't do that. If I did, it would kill us both. You
can rest assured that I will not harm you, my dear coyote." The
coyote thought for a while and then agreed to ferry the scorpion.
Halfway across the river, the scorpion reared up and stung the
coyote. With a shriek, the coyote yelled at the scorpion, "Why did
you do that? You've killed us both! What's wrong with you?" The
scorpion replied, "I'm a scorpion. I sting. What else would you
have expected of me?" The lesson of the story is that some people
simply are the way they are by nature, and they criticize and hurt
others. As spiritual leaders, whether pastoral or lay, we make ourselves the target of that criticism. To lead is to be criticized.

We aren't the first religious figures to be criticized. Moses
was criticized constantly by the Israelites wandering in the desert. Jesus was criticized not only by the Sadducees and Pharisees
but also by his followers. We forget that at one point Judas was
a supporter of Jesus, yet he became critical of Jesus and betrayed
him. Paul was criticized sharply by those complaining that he
was too conciliatory to the Gentiles, he hadn't been one of the
apostles in Jerusalem, and he wasn't a charismatic speaker like
another evangelist, Apollos.

Criticism isn't the problem, no matter how much it hurts. The
problem is our defensiveness in the face of criticism. We may be
criticized, but criticism has only the power we give it. If we become defensive, lashing out against those who criticize us, we've
lost the battle. I've discovered over the years that when we develop the ability to accept criticism, even that which we think
is unfair, and react with a sense of respect and care toward the
critic, it has the power to diminish the sting of the criticism.

Nevertheless, reacting to criticism without defensiveness is
hard. No one likes to be criticized, especially when the charge is
unfair. But's it's helpful to recognize that often the criticism flung
against us isn't necessarily *about* us. It's about the critic.

In the example cited above of the person who criticized me
over the drama ministry, I quickly realized that she wasn't upset with me because I didn't like the drama ministry. She was
upset that the ministry was no longer the sole strong ministry
of our church. Over the years our drama ministry has grown

stronger, along with most of our other ministries. Yet during the interim period before I came to Calvin Church, the drama and music ministries had held the church together. The ministries gave the church a sense of distinctiveness, cohesiveness, and success. When I came to the church, I worked to strengthen the drama ministry and all the others. The woman was upset not because I was against the ministry, but because in a relative sense it was no longer the main ministry. It was no longer the ministry around which all other church activities revolved. I also suspect that this woman didn't like me much because I was an authority figure—but that's a deeper issue. Again, the criticism wasn't really about me. It was about her, and the sooner I realized it, the more quickly I was able to put it in context and perspective.

Criticism not only tells us generally more about the critic than it does about ourselves, it also tells us what our limitations are. Frequently, congregational leaders, especially pastoral leaders, are criticized for not doing enough or more. We get criticized for many things: not visiting enough people, not visiting enough of the "right" people, not handling difficulties better, not being in our offices enough, not getting things done in time, not delivering better sermons, not understanding finances better, not having better-behaved children, not having a more involved spouse, and so many other things. There's no dearth of shortcomings to be criticized for. What these criticisms do tell us is that no matter how talented we are, we cannot do everything, nor should we do everything. And even if we were able to do everything at the church, where would our families and our personal lives be? I remember an older pastor telling me that during his career, he devoted his life to the church, but looking back he wished he had spent much more time with his family. He realized now that his wife and children needed him even more than the church did.

Over time I've found that the best attitude I can take toward criticism is to try my best to incarnate the advice from Dorotheos mentioned above, which is to receive criticism in a spirit of receptivity rather than defensiveness. I try my best to first consider how the person may be right. That doesn't mean that my first reaction won't be to defend myself. Sometimes self-defense just happens, but afterward I spend time reflecting and asking myself honestly if I have been wrong. After doing that, I may come to the conclusion that the critic is wrong and has an axe to grind, but I try my best to be open to the possibility that I am wrong. How do we become receptive? There are some practical guidelines:

- Let the person speak until she or he is done rather than interrupting.
- Make sure that my response is measured and calm in tone rather than nervous or angry.
- Ask questions to get more details about what the person is talking about instead of rushing to defend myself.
- Wait until the end of the tirade to explain my actions, and try my best to enlist the person as an ally in determining what I can do better in the future.

I remember doing these very things with the woman who called me complaining that she had been away for six weeks and that no one seemed to care. She was upset and decided that because of this mistreatment, it was time for her to look elsewhere for a church. I listened as best I could, trying to get clarity on what she was upset about and what she thought had happened. After a long time of listening, I explained that we thought we were being caring by giving her space. In the end, I offered to help her find another church where she could feel more cared about. I even offered to call the pastor of another church to ease the transition. By the end, I think she was appreciative. From time to time, I see her and we are friendly. Over time I also came to realize that whatever issues she had with the church and me, they had very little to do with the actual issue she had criticized me for. They had to do more with her expectations of the church, expectations we simply couldn't meet.

In the end, we need to accept criticism from others as part of the price we pay for leadership, doing our best not to take offense, and then find a way to provide support even if every cell in our bodies screams "No!" I believe that this is something of what it means to love our enemies and pray for those who persecute us (Matt. 5:44). When another criticizes us, for that moment the other becomes our enemy. How we respond determines the extent to which we move either toward reconciliation or toward defensiveness and division.

BECOME THANKFUL

In seven of the nine epistles written to particular churches, Paul begins by telling the people how thankful he is for them. We generally gloss over those remarkable openings in our rush to move onto the meat of the letter. In fact, if you consider 2 Corinthians part of a larger correspondence between Paul and the church at Corinth, begun in 1 Corinthians, eight out of nine letters begin with thanks. The only epistle he doesn't begin with thanksgiving is the epistle to the Galatians, and there are extenuating circumstances, such as the fact that the Galatians had turned away from the gospel. Paul had been criticized, severely criticized, by some of the churches, yet still he responds by telling them how thankful he is for them. For Paul, thankfulness was a crucial part of his leadership.

It is easy for us to lack gratitude and appreciation for our congregations and the members. We can get so focused either on our own agendas or plans, or on the extent to which members are or are not being involved, that we stop being thankful for them. Or we can become so consumed with the demands and tasks of our ministry and leadership that we never stop to be grateful for the ministry. As a result, lacking gratitude for those around us, we can become oblivious to them and what they actually do to contribute to the life of our congregations.

I believe that an essential aspect of humble leadership, an aspect that is both abstract and pragmatic, is gratitude. The word "gratitude" literally means to be in a state of "grace." To be "grateful" literally means to be full of grace. There is a connection between the extent to which we are grateful to God for our lives, vocations, and the others around us and the degree to which grace seems to flow into what we do. I believe that this flow of grace is reflected in Jesus's teaching to his disciples, "I am the vine, you are the branches. Those who abide in me and I in them bear much fruit, because apart from me you can do nothing"

(John 15:5). The implication is that just as the natural sap of a vine flows into the branches, the natural grace of Christ flows into and through us allowing us to bear fruit in our leadership.

Christian mystics throughout history have written about the connection between gratitude and blessing. The 15th-century mystic Thomas à Kempis said about the connection between gratitude and grace:

> So be grateful for every little gift and you will be worthy to receive greater ones. Consider the least gift as great and the most common as something special. If you consider the dignity of the giver, no gift will seem small or unimportant. Nothing given by the most high God is insignificant. And if he should send you pain and sorrow, you ought to be thankful, too, for whatever he permits he does for our own good. The person who wishes to keep God's grace should be thankful when it is given, and he should be patient when it is taken away. Pray for its return, then be cautious and humble lest it be lost.[5]

Thomas expresses an attitude that many today would question: a willingness to thank God for everything, *even the bad things*. But Thomas understood something that many modern Christians don't: even bad experiences can be grace-filled because they have the potential to transform us. Reflect on your life, and you'll discover a bad experience that actually had the effect of making you stronger, wiser, and better.

The modern mystic David Steindl-Rast recognizes how important gratefulness is:

> What counts on your path to fulfillment is that we remember the great truth that moments of surprise want to teach us: everything is gratuitous, everything is gift. The degree to which we are awake to this truth is the measure of our gratefulness. And gratefulness is the measure of our aliveness. . . .
>
> In moments when we are truly alive, we experience life as a gift. We also experience life as surprise.[6]

The extent to which we are grateful leaders is also the extent to which we open up to the surprises God has in store for us in the congregations we lead. I believe that as a rule, with some exceptions, congregations generally reflect their leaders. If we lead out of irritation, criticism, manipulation, and disappointment, then our congregations will reflect it by becoming cynical, wary, and divisive. If we are grateful, positive, appreciative leaders, our congregations will reflect those attitudes by becoming positive, hopeful, and open. I believe that one of the best things we can do as leaders is to ensure that our leadership is thankful, both to God for leading us where we are, and for the people we have the privilege of leading.

It's all too easy to take congregations, like our families, for granted. Perhaps we have bigger and better plans, and we see our congregations as mere stepping-stones. Perhaps we are disappointed that no bigger and better pastorate or other prestigious leadership post seems to be waiting in the wings. I don't know how many pastors I've worked with as a spiritual director who seem to be continually discontented with where they are. Yet the one constant I've noticed is that when they change their attitude toward their congregations, their congregations change.

So how do we become more thankful in a practical way? I believe that the main way to become thankful is intentionally to look around our congregations with a sense of practical appreciation. To appreciate something means to see the value in it, while to depreciate something means to diminish what value there is. The practical exercise I do is to stop at times and look at the situation I am in, the staff I am surrounded by, the leaders I work with, and to look at what is really good and wonderful about them. Just doing this exercise has led me to several conclusions, the first of which is that I work with the best staff members that can be found anywhere. I don't know whether I am right about this, but I believe it and I see it. Because I believe, I see. I'm sure that I could look at them and see what is wrong with them, but I don't. I try my best to see what is right about them. And it makes all the difference. I look at the lay leaders we have, and have had, over the years, and it is easy to see what is right and wonderful about them when I focus on that. I don't focus on how they may not have come through. Instead, I focus on how they *have* come through. And I focus on them as people, trying my best to see what is good and wonderful about them. It's amazing how this attitude can change relationships and interactions. I had to teach myself this approach because as a counselor I had been trained to see what is wrong with people. Paying attention to what is right with people has been a revelation because it has allowed me to see the good in people, even in those who aren't always that good.

I do the same with the congregation. I believe that Calvin Church is the best church anywhere. I don't know if I am right about this, but I believe it, and I believe that believing it makes it so. There are times when I stand in front of my congregation, and I am immensely thankful that God has put me here. I don't want to give you any illusions. If you choose to come to Calvin Church, you could find plenty wrong with it. But what's wrong with it is not my focus. My focus is not only to see what's right about it but to also see the potential in it that can make it even better.

Leading out of gratitude, appreciation, and thankfulness is a practical and pragmatic practice. And it is powerful in the way it can transform a congregation.

FROM PRAXIS BACK TO PRINCIPLE

There are a multitude of little practical things that can be done to improve our leadership and make it more humble, to make it more open to God's guidance and providence. Yet what I've just outlined are five practical practices that I believe can yield tremendous results and transform a church. Surrounding ourselves with good people and letting them shine is crucial to humble leadership because it allows others to become the focus of ministry rather than us. Too often we lead out of ego and pride, which results in our needing to be the center of a church or ministry, whether we are a pastor or a lay leader. Yet taking pride in the shining of others enhances communal leadership tremendously. It allows ministry to grow exponentially.

Leading in a way that encourages others to contribute to leadership and to move together as one is also crucial. Too often individual leaders want to be the "deciders," but the creative leadership I've seen is always collaborative. Collaborative leadership allows the voice of the Spirit to speak more thoroughly through many voices. In the end, collaborative leadership requires the willingness to stop talking and to make a decision, yet the decisions have the potential to be creative and Spirit-filled. It is humble leadership because it shares authority without giving up authority. We remain open to God, while also having the courage to lead with conviction.

To be a leader who is able to give guidance and let go also requires a tremendous humility because it means willingly taking a backseat to other leaders without relinquishing leadership. This may sound confusing, but in simple terms, letting others be responsible for their areas of ministry means trusting others to do well, even if they don't. It is unifying leadership because it creates the conditions for other leaders to contribute.

Accepting criticism, resisting offense, and providing support are extremely difficult things to do as a leader. They call for not only a great sense of humility but also for a great sense of personal integrity. They require us to be able to be attacked by another without allowing the other to define and diminish us. I have a rule when I am severely criticized. I have three days to get over it. The first day I can obsess about it. The second day I begin to relinquish it. By the third day I have to quit being a baby and return to normal life. It is hard to keep to the schedule with especially harsh criticism, but by doing so, I am being realistic in two ways. First, I recognize that any criticism is what psychologists call a "narcissistic injury," meaning an "ego bruise," and it is hard to recover quickly from the pain, just as it can be hard to recover from a physical bruise. But as with a physical bruise, I also have to let the injury heal and move on. Just as an athlete cannot let a bruise keep him out of the game for long, neither can we let an ego bruise keep us from serving God. We have to patch it up as best we can and move on. Sometimes bruises can be especially deep, but we have to do our best. If the bruise goes too deep, then we may need to see a counselor or spiritual director to help us heal. This step, again, requires the humility to let go of the need to be impervious to assault, and to accept that sometimes we get assaulted and need the help of another to overcome the assault. It doesn't mean that the critic is right.

Finally, becoming grateful in our leadership is crucial because it enhances those around us. When we are able, in the words of 1 Thessalonians, to give thanks in all circumstances (1 Thess. 5:18), our gratitude allows us to bring out the good in any situation. Being grateful in all circumstances can be hard, especially in troublesome situations, but if we can find things for which to be grateful to God, we can discover God deeply with us in every aspect of leadership.

Notes

CHAPTER 1: HUMBLE LEADERSHIP

1. Louis Fischer, *The Life of Mahatma Gandhi* (San Francisco: Harper & Row, 1950).

2. Dorotheos of Gaza, *Discourses and Sayings,* trans. Eric P. Wheeler (Kalamazoo, Mich.: Cistercian Publications, 1977), 145-146.

3. Thomas R. Kelly, *A Testament of Devotion* (San Francisco: HarperSanFrancisco, 1992), 35-36.

4. Thomas à Kempis, *The Imitation of Christ,* trans. William C. Creasy (Notre Dame, Ind.: Ave Maria Press, 1989), 30-31.

5. Jim Collins, *Good to Great* (San Francisco: HarperCollins, 2001), 3.

6. Ibid., 12-13.

CHAPTER 2: SELF-AWARE LEADERSHIP

1. N. Graham Standish, *Becoming a Blessed Church: Forming a Church of Spiritual Purpose, Presence, and Power* (Herndon, Va.: Alban Institute, 2005), chapter 2.

2. Teresa of Avila, *The Way of Perfection* (New York: Image Books, 1991), 258-259.

3. C. S. Lewis, *The Screwtape Letters* (New York: Touchstone Books, 1996), 58.

4. The insights and descriptions about personality disorders and traits are adapted from the *Diagnostic and Statistical Manual of Mental Disorders-IV-TR* (Washington, D.C.: American Psychiatric Association, 2000), 685-789; and Gregory W. Lester, *Personality Disorders in Social Work Practice* (Denver: Heritage Professional Education, LLC, 1998).

5. Thomas H. Green, S.J., *Weeds Among the Wheat: Discernment: Where Prayer and Action Meet* (Notre Dame, Ind.: Ave Maria Press, 1984).

CHAPTER 3: PRAYERFUL LEADERSHIP

1. The following descriptions are from events depicted in the film *Romero*, Elwood E. Kieser, producer; John Duigan, director; Paulist Pictures, 1989.

2. Quote taken from the "Resources for Catholic Education" Web site, Gilles Cote, producer. http://www.silk.net/RelEd/ezineromero.htm

3. Nicole Casta, "Robertson called for the assassination of Venezuela's president" (Washington, D.C.: Media Matters for America Web site, http://mediamatters.org (accessed August 22, 2005).

4. Adrian van Kaam, *Traditional Formation: Formative Spirituality*, vol. 5 (New York: Crossroad Publishing, 1992), 271.

5. The following are excellent resources to help develop practices of prayer: Richard J. Foster, *Celebration of Discipline* (San Francisco: Harper & Row, 1988); Richard J. Foster, *Prayer* (San Francisco: Harper & Row, 1992); Evelyn Underhill, *Life as Prayer* (Harrisburg, Pa.: Morehouse Publishing, 1991); Thomas Keating, *Open Mind, Open Heart* (New York: Continuum, 1992); and N. Graham Standish, *Discovering the Narrow Path* (Louisville: Westminster John Knox, 2002).

6. Brother Lawrence, *The Practice of the Presence of God*, trans. Robert J. Edmonson (Brewster, Mass.: Paraclete Press, 1985), 89-90.

7. Kelly, *A Testament of Devotion*, 8.

8. Gerald May, *Will and Spirit* (San Francisco: Harper & Row, 1982), 6.

9. Robert Aitken and David Steindl-Rast, *The Ground We Share: Everyday Practice, Buddhist and Christian* (Ligouri, Mo: Triumph Books, 1994), 71.

10. Danny E. Morris and Charles M. Olsen, *Discerning God's Will Together: A Spiritual Practice For The Church* (Bethesda: Alban Institute, 1997); Roy M. Oswald and Robert Friedrich, Jr., *Discerning Your Congregation's Future* (Bethesda: Alban Institute, 1996); Ben Campbell Johnson, *Discerning God's Will* (Louisville: Westminster John Knox, 1990); and Luke Timothy Johnson, *Scripture and Discernment: Decision Making in the Church* (Nashville: Abingdon, 1996).

11. Hannah Hurnard, *Hinds' Feet on High Places* (Wheaton, Ill.: Living Books, 1975), 59. Quotation used by permission of Tyndale House Publishers, Inc..

CHAPTER 4: UNIFYING LEADERSHIP

1. David Horowitz, "I'm a Uniter, Not a Divider," in *Salon.com* (San Francisco: Salon Media Group, Inc., May 6, 1999), http://www.salon.com/news/feature/1999/05/06/bush

2. "Poll: Nation Split on Bush as Uniter or Divider," *CNN.com* (Atlanta: CNN) http://www.cnn.com/2005/ALLPOLITICS/01/19/poll

3. "Memorable quotes from 'The 700 Club,'" (Internet Movie Database [IMDb]) http://www.imdb.com/title/tt0149408/quotes

4. This and other generational descriptions are based on William Strauss and Neil Howe, *Generation: The History of America's Future, 1584 to 2069* (New York: Quill/William Morrow & Company, 1991).

5. Hannah Whitall Smith, *The Christian's Secret of a Happy Life* (Grand Rapids: Spire Books, 1952), 71.

6. Richard Boyatzis and Annie McKee, *Resonant Leadership* (Cambridge, Mass.: Harvard Business School Press, 2005), 6.

7. Ibid., 4.

8. Ibid., 77.

9. Ibid., 16.

10. Benedict of Nursia, *The Rule of St. Benedict,* trans. Anthony C. Meisel and M. L. del Mastro (New York: Image Books, 1975).

CHAPTER 5: SPIRIT-LED LEADERSHIP

1. Bill Easum, *Leadership on the OtherSide* (Nasville: Abingdon Press, 2000), 46-64.

2. Ibid., 46.

3. Ibid., 57.

4. Stephen Covey, *The Seven Habits of Highly Effective People: Powerful Lessons in Personal Change* (New York: Free Press, 1989), 71.

5. Ibid., 78.

6. Ibid., 78.

7. Ibid., 81.

8. Ibid., 82.

9. Ibid., 83.

10. Ibid., 83

11. Ibid., 93.

12. Standish, *Becoming a Blessed Church,* 15.

13. *Star Wars: The Empire Strikes Back* (Lucasfilm, Ltd., 20th Century Fox DVD, 2004), scene 31, "There Is No Try."

14. Prayer of Patrick of Ireland, from *Book of Common Worship* (Louisville: Westminster John Knox, 1993), 27.

15. Boyatzis and McKee, *Resonant Leadership,* 28.

16. Jean-Pierre de Caussade, *The Sacrament of the Present Moment,* trans. Kitty Muggeridge (San Francisco: HarperSanFrancisco, 1989), 18.

17. Adrian van Kaam, *Formative Spirituality, Volume One: Fundamental Formation* (New York: Crossroads, 1989), 263.

18. As quoted in Roy Lawrence, *Christian Healing Rediscovered: A Guide to Spiritual, Mental, Physical Wholeness* (Downers Grove, Ill.: InterVarsity, 1980), 104.

19. Frank Laubach, *Brother Lawrence: Practicing His Presence* (Sargent, Ga.: The SeedSowers, 1973), 5.

20. Henry T. Blackaby and Claude V. King, *Experiencing God* (Nashville: Broadman and Holman Publishers, 1994), 50.

21. Ibid.

22. Ibid.

CHAPTER 6: HUMBLY EFFECTIVE LEADERSHIP

1. Collins, *Good to Great,* 12-13.

2. Ibid., 18.

3. Wess Roberts and Bill Ross, *Make It So: Leadership Lessons from Star Trek: The Next Generation* (Pocket Books: New York, 1995).

4. Dorotheos of Gaza, *Discourses and Sayings,* 140-147.

5. Thomas à Kempis, *The Imitation of Christ,* 76.

6. David Steindl-Rast, *Gratefulness: The Heart of Prayer* (New York: Paulist Press, 1984), 12.